Origins:
The Road to the
Messiah

By

Sidney Neal Greene

This book was printed in the United States of America.

To order additional copies of this book contact:

Sidney Neal Greene
Pound, VA
sidneynealgreene@gmail.com

FWB

Table of Contents

Purpose

Origins: The Road to the Messiah is an easy-to-understand book designed to increase the faith of junior high, high school and college-age youth, as well as parents, teachers, professors, and those who work with young people. In the first portion of this book we will discuss the differences between creation and evolution. Evolution teaches that there is no God, and all things came into existence by chance over a period of billions of years. We will examine this theory to see if it is even possible. We will look at many examples of God's perfect creation abilities – many from science itself. We will then take up the Genesis account of creation by examining the first 2 Chapters of Genesis, whose title means "beginning" or "origin." In these 2 Chapters, we will see how many of the things in our world originated. In great detail, we will examine Chapter 3, in which we have the account of the fall of man and how sin entered the world. The most important part of this book is Verse 15. In this Verse, God tells us how He would redeem sinful man though His "seed," His Son, the Messiah. If not for this promise, it would not matter what anyone believes about creation. From this point, we will begin following the Bible narrative of the fulfillment of this verse. It is called "The Road to the Messiah -- a dark and bloody road with much sin and much violence. We will follow this road through Genesis 25, finishing up this book with the story of Abraham's son, Isaac.

Scattered throughout the Chapters are *Creation Moments*, transcripts from a daily, 2-minute radio broadcast heard on over 1300 radio stations. On their website, Creation Moments states that "in a world bombarded by false messages about origins, Creation Moments provides accurate, up-to-date information about new discoveries in God's creation and how they relate to the Bible. We believe true science backs Biblical truth." In this book, we have chosen to include transcripts about bats, and the sun, moon, and stars. You should like those!

Origins: The Road to the Messiah concludes with a Chapter specifically designed to address how students, parents, teachers, and professors should respond to the material discussed.

Introduction

Imagine that you suddenly found yourself in this world, fully grown. You had never existed before. You look around and notice a multitude of animals and insects in the grass and on the hills. You hear, then see, birds flying above you. There are all kinds of trees laden with fruit, berry bushes, and plants for you to eat. As your belly begins to growl, you see that there are other people with you -- friends, family members, and strangers. As you explore, you realize you have the ability to think, to feel, and to act. You have a personality and abilities that are uniquely your own. As you watch the other people around you, you see that they are also unique as individuals, with their own thoughts and feelings. The one thing all of you would be wondering is, "Where did I come from?" and "Who made all these wonderful things?" and "How did we get to this beautiful and intriguing place?" As intelligent, thinking, and unique individuals, you would never entertain the thought that you were the product of chance. You would know that something material cannot come from nothing. Each of you would obviously be looking for a word from whoever put you here -- your Creator or creators. You would want to meet him and ask, "Why did you create us and what do you expect, if anything, in return?" This is precisely what this book is all about.

Today, a theory called evolution, which says there is no God and everything came into existence by blind chance, is overwhelming our culture. There are people from every walk of life and every sector of society who hold to this theory. It is having a devastating effect on all people but primarily our young people in high school and college. As a result of so many individuals not knowing or seeking to know where they came from, society is trying to find themselves through sinful acts. Sexual immorality is growing worse and worse. Murder, drug addiction, and the destruction of the family home are happening more and more. The confidence of even those who believe in creation is being shaken and causing many to fall away from the truth. Thru the Bible Radio is radio series in which teacher, J. Vernon McGee, takes listeners through the entire Bible in a 5-year period. In one program introduction, the host, Steve Shwetz, comments, "When Charles Darwin published his book On the Origin of Species in 1859, he set off a new wave of thinking that radically altered the world view of scientists, educators, and the organized church. Within a few decades, entire denominations had rejected the biblical account of creation. Adam and Eve became mythological characters symbolic of man's ascent from primordial slime. It was onward and upward toward a brave new world. .. Just the opposite is true. Beginning at the Garden of Eden, man has descended down into a cesspool of depravity and perversion." The pressure to doubt God's creation and yield to the theory of evolution is so great that many Christian schools and Christian colleges are teaching some form of it. Dr. John MacArthur, president of the Master's Bible College and Seminary in California, says that the Master's College is one of a coalition of over 100 Bible colleges and all but 6 are teaching evolution.

God gave each of us a brain for analyzing information. We should use it when we hear the theory of evolution being presented on the Internet, in books, magazines, or other media. We should use our brain when we are in a classroom and we hear teachers or professors presenting a theory that is totally, absolutely impossible. And so we begin.

Chapter 1

The Bible is Our Guide: The Origin of All Truth

But don't you worry -- The truth about all this, along with the explanation as to why we are here in this world, has been given to us in a book we call the Bible. This book not only tells us how we got here, but more importantly, where we as believers in Jesus Christ are going. John 17:3, "And this is eternal life, that they know You the only true God and Jesus Christ whom you have sent."

In the front of many Bibles is this quotation from an unknown author: "This book (the Word of God) contains: the mind of God, the state of man, the way of salvation, the doom of sinners, and the happiness of believers. Its doctrine is holy, its precepts are binding, its histories are true, and its decisions are immutable. Read it to be wise, believe it to be saved, and practice it to be holy. It contains light to direct you, food to support you, and comfort to cheer you. It is the traveler's map, the pilgrim's staff, the pilot's compass, the soldier's sword, and the Christian's charter. Here heaven is open, and the gates of hell are disclosed. Christ is the grand subject, our good its design, and the glory of God its end. It should fill the memory, rule the heart, and guide the feet. Read it slowly, frequently, and prayerfully. It is a mine of wealth, health to the soul, and a river of pleasure. It is given to you here in this life, will be opened at the judgment, and is established forever. It involves the highest responsibility, will reward the greatest labor, and condemn all who trifle with its contents."

Let's first delve into our discussion with a particularly interesting Creation Moment about bats. Ask yourself honestly "Could this happen by chance?"

A "Creation Moment":
Evolution of Bats Gets Monkeyed Up

Psalm 33:6
"By the word of the LORD were the heavens made; and all the host of them by the breath of his mouth."

We have noted many times the different ways in which bats defy evolutionary explanations. For their echolocation systems to evolve, bats had to develop simultaneously the ability to make high pitched sounds, hear those sounds, and figure out what they mean. How did they eat before they evolved these abilities? Then there is the problem of evolving typical mammalian forearms into bat wings without crippling the creature in the process. Even evolutionists admit that the evolution of all these features even once is highly unlikely.

Bats are divided into two sub orders. Smaller bats, like the free tail bats of Mexico, are classified in the sub order of Microchiroptera. Large bats, like the fruit bat, are  classified into the sub order of Megachiroptera. The brains of the larger bats have very different visual pathways than those in smaller bats. The visual pathways of the larger bats are more like those of primates! But no evolutionist would dare suggest that they evolved from primates. The second complication is that this means that both small and large bats could not have evolved from a common ancestor. It further means that all the unlikely features of bats had to have evolved at least twice, if evolution were true.

The Bible offers a simple explanation for the design of the bat and the differences between their brains. They were made by God using whatever designs He knew would be best for that creature's way of life, without regard for later, humanly devised classification systems.

Prayer:
Lord, thank You for Your Word that made life and gives life now. Amen.

Notes:

"Bats: Sophistication in Miniature," Creation, 12/98 2/99, pp. 28 31. Photo: Giant golden crowned fruit bat. Courtesy of LDC, Inc. Foundation. (CC-BY-SA 3.0)

Chapter 2

A Simple Experiment

(3 tails, 3 heads, or mixed)

Try a simple experiment. Take three coins and lay them in one hand. With the other hand, take one coin out and lay it down before looking at it. Take out another and lay it beside the first. Do the same with the third. See if there is an order, like all three are heads up or all three are heads down. The first time I attempted this, it took 17 tries just to get three coins in a particular order.

On my next attempt, it took 27; on my final one, it took 4. So, with just 3 coins, it may take any number of attempts to have them in a particular order – all by chance. If it is this hard to get 3 coins in order, imagine what the odds would be for the following scientific fact to happen by sheer chance:

> Dr. Jerry Bergman, professor of science at Ohio's Northwest College states, "At the moment of conception, a fertilized human egg is about the size of a pinhead. Yet it contains information equivalent to about six billion 'chemical letters.' This is enough information to fill 1,000 books, 500 pages thick with print so small you would need a microscope to read it! If all the chemical letters in the human body were printed in books, it is estimated they would fill the Grand Canyon fifty times!"

To think that this could happen by coincidence or luck goes far beyond imagination or possibility, yet scientists who advocate evolution as blind chance would have us believe that this is what happens. We only used 3 coins in our simple experiment. If we keep adding coins, the chances of coming out with all heads or all tails increases exponentially. Imagine 6 billion little things!

Take just one cell of our body. This cell gets the information as to what its function is from its DNA code. Every kind of cell has its own code, or to simplify, its own job description written in DNA. A liver cell, for instance, has a liver code. All the liver cells work together to perform the function of a liver. Kidney cells work together to perform the function of a kidney. After consulting a number of reliable book and Internet sources, I have found that, if the DNA in any one cell were uncoiled, it would be a strip approximately 6 – 7 feet long, and if there are anywhere from 37 to 100 trillion cells in the human body, how long would your DNA be? You do the math. This blows my little mind. Does it yours? We couldn't make 1 cell, let alone trillions of them. As we keep using our brain, we think: "Where did this DNA in these cells in a human body come from?" "What gives them the energy to complete their daily jobs? "What reads all that information on the DNA?"

Some Amazing Facts

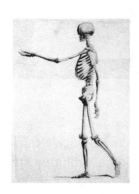

One of the things Darwinists like to do is criticize the way in which God made things. In his book *Darwin on Trial*, Phil Johnson discussed some of Harvard Professor Steven J. Gould's writings. Gould informed creation scientists that the skeletal systems of certain animals, like rats, bats, porpoises, and man are very poorly engineered. He implied that if our Creator really exists then he must not be very smart. He stated, "An engineer, starting from scratch, could design better limbs in each case."

Can any of us build a tiny skeleton the size a newborn baby would have? Can we then make the bones of that skeleton grow as a person grows into an adult? If a bone is damaged or broken, can we make one that can repair itself? Our Creator can do it. He does it every day.

Consider the amazing engineering of the hand. The tasks we can do with our fingers and thumb are almost limitless. We can do the tiniest and most delicate work like threading a needle or using a pair of tweezers to pull out a tiny splinter. We can hold and pound with a hammer or we can open and close a pair of scissors. We can pick up and carry ALL our groceries into the house in just one trip!

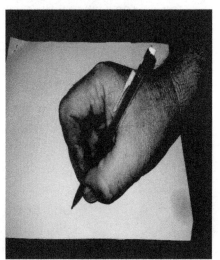

What about the length of a male peacock's tail? Their tails are sometimes 6 feet long! Some evolutionists criticize this saying that the tail inhibits the peacock's ability to escape predators. (How have peacocks survived this long?) They say that if a Creator does exist, he would not make this mistake. God does not make mistakes. The peacock's tail is created the way it is because that is the way God wanted it. Scientists cannot create one cell, but they think that they are smarter than God, Who is able to make all the trillions of cells in our bodies "ex nihilo," Latin for "out of nothing."

It is absolutely awesome to read about some of the things that living creatures can do – without any training.

Baby birds, for instance, know from the time they hatch how to build a nest, lay their eggs in it, and hatch then raise their own young. Do they acquire this knowledge by chance or does God put this knowledge into their DNA?

What about the incredible dance of honey bees as they communicate to each other the location of a source of food? A bee finds a field of clover flowers. She returns to the hive and begins to rotate and wiggle. The other bees watch as the dancer communicates the exact location and distance to a food source. Baby bees know how to do this without any training from adult bees.

One final thought: *Take the 3 coins mentioned earlier and look at them before you lay them down. You decide if the heads or tails should be up. You can place them in any order you want. You have absolute control. So does our Creator.*

Chapter 3

Absolutes

Let's talk about a word mentioned just above, the word "absolute." Various dictionaries define the word as "perfect in quality or nature; complete; not mixed; not limited by restrictions or exceptions; a value or principle that is regarded as universally valid or that may be viewed without relation to other things;" and finally, "that which exists without being dependent on anything else."

One example of an absolute would be a measuring tape. All measuring tapes are absolutely the same — or are supposed to be. They are made with marked inches and fractions of inches. Twelve inches equal 1 foot, 24 inches equals 2 feet, etc. -- most everyone knows that. In the building of a house, you have several craftsmen working together. There are carpenters, roofers, plumbers, electricians, and trim and molding craftsmen. The one tool they all use is a measuring tape. Each worker may use a tape of various size or length, but all of them have tapes are absolute in that they have the exact same increments for measuring. Suppose that the carpenters have a tape that is different than the plumbers which have one that is different from the electricians. Let's say the carpenter's foot is 16 inches, the plumbers have a 10-inch foot, and the electricians have their own tape in which 1 foot measures 6 inches. Imagine what a house would look like if this were the case. It would be impossible to have a house that was square and plumb and even look like anything resembling one. The windows and doors would not fit. The electricity or plumbing would not work. Total chaos would be the result. Each worker may have tools that are specifically designed for his trade, but the one tool for measuring, the tape, has to be absolutely the same for all.

We move on to discuss two instances of absolutes that were ignored or broken and both resulted in severe consequences. The first is a practical one from the field of aviation. The second is a moral one from the Bible.

In the early days of aviation, there were numerous plane crashes that occurred when a pilot flew into fog or a storm and lost his visibility. He was depending on his sense of sight and his proprioceptive sense (a sense that perceives the body's own position, motion, and state) to guide him to his destination. Without being able to see around him, something would happen to the fluid in his inner ear that kept him oriented and balanced. As a result, many pilots were killed. Instruments were subsequently invented and installed in airplane cockpits. These instruments were absolutes; they stayed the same whether the weather was rainy, or foggy, or clear. These instruments would help the pilot keep the plane flying safely. Pilots had to be trained on the use of them -- the instruments which showed altitude, position of the plane, level flight, and speed. By keeping his eyes on these instruments, a pilot could fly into the densest fog or worst storm, clear it, and still be able to land safely.

One day, some years ago, a certain pilot called the control tower and asked for help as he had gotten disoriented due to heavy fog. The tower asked him if he had instruments on his plane and did he know how to use them. He answered that he had had training and knew how to use his instruments. Unfortunately, he kept his focus on the fog. The tower could only watch as his plane began to spin out of control. His cries for help were pitiful. He crashed into the ground, killing not only him, but his 3 passengers. Years later, a test pilot who was flying a new plane got a message from the tower. There was another plane lost in a storm. Could he find the lost plane and bring him in? Using his radar he quickly found it and moved to the front of it. As he spoke to his fellow pilot, his instructions were simple, "Sir, just keep your eyes focused on the lights on the back of my plane and follow me in." Both pilots' cockpit instruments were absolute. The test pilot knew his plane and trusted what he was seeing on the control panel and was flying by what his instruments told him. The lost pilot did not trust his instruments. In the end, happily, both planes made safe landings. The lost plane would have crashed if there had not been someone to guide it, someone who trusted in absolutes.

Our second example of absolutes is from the Bible. Over 4,000 years ago God gave His people a group of guidelines called the 10 Commandments.

God spoke all these words in Exodus 20:
"I am the Lord your God, who brought you out of the land of Egypt, out of the house of slavery.

"You shall have no other gods before Me.

"You shall not make for yourself an idol, or any likeness of what is in heaven above or on the earth beneath or in the water under the earth. You shall not worship them or serve them; for I, the Lord your God, am a jealous God visiting the iniquity of the fathers on the children, on the third and the fourth generations of those who hate Me, but showing loving kindness to thousands, to those who love Me and keep My commandments.

"You shall not take the name of the Lord your God in vain, for the Lord will not leave him unpunished who takes His name in vain.

"Remember the Sabbath day, to keep it holy. Six days you shall labor and do all your work, but the seventh day is a Sabbath of the Lord your God; in it you shall not do any work, you or your son or your daughter, your male or your female servant or your cattle or your sojourner who stays with you. For in six days the Lord made the heavens and the earth, the sea and all that is in them, and rested on the seventh day; therefore the Lord blessed the Sabbath day and made it holy.

"Honor your father and your mother, that your days may be prolonged in the land which the Lord your God gives you.
"You shall not murder.
"You shall not commit adultery.
"You shall not steal.
"You shall not bear false witness against your neighbor.

"You shall not covet your neighbor's house; you shall not covet your neighbor's wife or his male servant or his female servant or his ox or his donkey or anything that belongs to your neighbor."

Along with blessings for obeying these laws, penalties and consequences were recorded in later Bible chapters and books. The death penalty was the outcome for disobedience to many of them.

About 1,000 years after God gave His people the 10 Commandments, a king came to Israel's throne. Second Samuel tells us that his name was David. At one point during his reign (the narrative is found in Chapter 11), David was on the roof of his palace and saw a woman on the roof of a nearby house bathing. His army was away, gone out on a campaign to battle with the enemies of Israel. David should have been with his men as was expected. This would have saved him and many others from years of terrible pain and suffering.

The woman bathing was named Bathsheba. She was married to one of David's mighty fighting men. His name was Uriah. King David looked and looked and began to lust after this woman. David broke No. 10 of God's absolute commandments that said, "You shall not covet your neighbor's wife." He sent for her and wound up in bed with her thus breaking another commandment – No. 7 "You shall not commit adultery."

One day Bathsheba sent word to David, "I am with child." David sent for her husband to come home from the battle and have a mini vacation with his wife. The warrior Uriah was a loyal man full of integrity. He is one of my favorite men in the Bible. He refused to go sleep in his house but slept on the ground at his front door instead. When David found that Uriah did not sleep in his house, David asked him why. Uriah said to David, "The ark and Israel and Judah are staying in temporary shelters, and my lord Joab and the servants of my lord are camping in the open field. Shall I then go to my house to eat and drink and sleep with my wife? By your life and the life of your soul I will not do such a thing." David asked him to stay another night. He got Uriah drunk, but he still did not go down to his house. When this did not work, he sent Uriah back to the army with a letter to his commander, Joab. The letter contained instructions to carry out Uriah's own death sentence. David knew that there was no chance that Uriah would read the letter. The letter had these instructions for Joab: "Put Uriah on the front line, and in the hottest part of the battle, and withdraw the rest of the army from him." Uriah, not being able to take on the enemy by himself, nevertheless followed his general's command and paid for it with his life. Later, the prophet Nathan came and reminded David that God had been watching everything he had done. David cried out his confession, "I have sinned against God."

That is what always happens when someone lies, steals, murders, commits adultery or breaks any of God's laws. Their sins are really against God. The penalty for

David's sin called for his death, but God put away David's sin so that David would not die. However, God did pronounce severe penalties for his sin. The child that Bathsheba bore became sick and died even after David fasted and prayed for a week. We can imagine that every time David saw Bathsheba, it reminded him what he had done to a faithful and loyal man and his wife. David would have been better off if *he* had died because of what subsequently happened to others in his family. Briefly, his son Amnon lusted after his own sister, Tamar. (She was actually his half-sister as David had children by another wife. The sin of polygamy, which was practiced by men in those days, was never condoned by God. It caused lust among family members, sometimes kings had their own sons murdered, and brothers often killed each other as they fought to be the one to succeed to their father's throne.) Amnon was so love (lust) sick for his beautiful sister that he tricked her into bringing him food to eat. As soon as they were alone, he raped her even though she pleaded with him not to disgrace her. After he had finished his evil deed, he hated her and ordered her out. But she said to him, "No, because this wrong in sending me away is greater than the other you have done to me. But he had his young men who attended him to throw her out." (2 Samuel 13)

Now Tamar had a full brother named Absalom. Absalom soon found out what Amnon had done to his sister. He told her to keep quiet about what had happened and encouraged her not to take this matter to heart. She remained with Absalom and moved into his house, so desolate she refused to see anyone. Absalom waited about

2 years and did not speak either good or bad to Amnon. He sat a trap for Amnon by inviting him to a party with all the king's sons. When Amnon was drunk, Absalom had his servants put him to death.

David's sin paid out one more horrible consequence. Absalom started an uprising to take over his father's throne. David and his loyal followers had to flee from him. The day came when these two forces met in battle. David expressly pleaded with his men not to harm Absalom, but Joab, David's commander, found Absalom caught by his long hair in the fork of an oak tree and Joab killed him. When David found out that Absalom was dead, he became terribly grief stricken. The account of what happened is recorded in 2 Samuel 18 and 19. David knew that Absalom was not saved and had no hope for his salvation.

Galatians 6:7 gives this warning, "Do not be deceived, God is not mocked; for whatever a man sows, this he will also reap." On the practical side, there is an old saying "Chickens come home to roost." These truths are illustrated by looking at the life of a person who spends his or her time drinking alcohol, taking drugs, showing greed, being disobedient to their parents, being untrustworthy, etc. (See Romans 1). The day will come when the seeds they have sown will grow up and the consequences can be terrible indeed.

Chapter 4

In The Beginning: Order or Chance?

God has absolute control.

Genesis 1:1 states, "In the beginning God created the heavens and the earth." This is an absolute statement. It either happened this way or it did not. If not, then the only other explanation is that all things came into existence by blind, impersonal chance. There was some kind of matter that existed in the universe (and where did that come from?) and out of that came the earth, with its life; the sun; the stars; and the rest of our solar system. Scientists call this explanation the "Big Bang Theory." But is this possible?

Creation scientists and evolution scientists both believe in a big bang that brought the universe into existence. The difference in their theories is that creation scientists believe it could not have happened without a Creator Who had the power and intelligence to do it. The God of the Bible tells us He did it. He does not tell us how He did it or where He got His power and intelligence. We could not comprehend it anyway.

Dr. Jeff Miller is the full-time science writer at Apologetics Press. In his article "The Five Manifestations of

Natural Phenomena," he stated: "So, time, force, action, space, and matter are the five manifestations of all scientific phenomena ... This truth—fundamental to understanding science—was articulated by an agnostic in the 19th century, and yet these fundamental principles were articulated in the very first verse of the Bible millennia ago. 'In the beginning [time], God [force] created [action] the heavens [space] and the Earth [matter]'." Who was this agnostic? It was the staunch evolutionist Herbert Spencer (1820-1903). Miller continues, "It is truly amazing that a renowned apostle of agnosticism would be the one to verbally articulate this discovery from science—a discovery which gives significant weight to the contention that one can know there is a God and that the Bible is His inspired Word. And further, it is notably ironic that the very man from whom Charles Darwin took the phrase, "survival of the fittest" (Spencer, 1864, 2:444), would be the man that unknowingly found evidence specifically supporting the inspiration of Genesis chapter one—the very chapter of the Bible that relates the truth about man's origin. Acts 14:17 rightly says, "Nevertheless He did not leave Himself without witness, in that He did good...'."

John 1:3 is talking about Jesus: "All things came into being through Him, and apart from Him nothing came into being that has come into being." Not only the Bible, but creation itself with all the clouds and rain and rivers and mountains and volcanoes and ..... Give evidence of a wise, powerful Creator. This is the only possible explanation.

Chapter 5

Man Is Without Excuse

The world is full of people who do not have access to a Bible. What about them? Are they going to be accountable for their beliefs? Let's look at some of the ways God has manifested Himself or shown that He is around. The main way is what we have just discussed -- through His written word. Second, creation itself speaks of the existence of God. Romans 1:19 says, "That which is known about God is evident within them; for God made it evident through creation." And finally, He has written in the heart of man that there is a God. No one can use the excuse that they have not heard of God or have evidence of His existence. Anywhere you go in this world, from the heart of the darkest jungles in Africa and South America to people living in the Arctic Circle, the peoples have one thing in common -- they know in their heart that there is a God. But rather than acknowledge what they clearly know in their mind and observe with their eyes, they turn from worshiping the true and living God to the worship of animals, images of creatures or themselves. They choose to walk away from the light God reveals to them to a dark world where they can make their own religion and its accompanying laws and rules.

Romans 1:24, 25 says, "Therefore God gave them over in the lusts of their hearts to impurity so their bodies would be dishonored among them. For they exchanged the truth of God for a lie, and worshiped and served the creature rather than the Creator who is blessed forever. Amen."

So, how does this happen? There are four pertinent examples of this fact found in the Bible. Here is the first. In the book of Exodus, God had called Moses to lead the children of Israel out of Egypt to the land God had promised to Abraham, Isaac, and Jacob. God told Abraham that the children of Israel would spend 400 years in Egypt. Pharaoh, the king of Egypt, would not let the people go, so God used Moses to smite the earth with plagues. One of the Egyptian gods was struck by God every time Pharaoh refused to let the people go.

In the second example, we have a group of people called the Philistines. They worshiped a carved god called Dagon. When the Philistines captured the ark of the covenant of God, they brought it into Dagon's temple. The next morning, Dagon had fallen over. They set him back up. The following morning, he had fallen over again. This time, his head and the palms of his hands were cut off and only the trunk of his body remained. (1 Samuel 5)

Thirdly, there was a god that was heavily worshipped by many people groups, even many of the people of God, called Baal. First Kings 18 gives the details of a contest between Baal and Elijah the prophet who knew and served the only true and living God. Baal would not answer his priests by sending fire down to consume a sacrifice, but Elijah's God burnt up the sacrificial offering, the wood, the stones of the altar, the dust and even 12 jars of water that had been poured over the sacrifice.

Finally, there was a horrible god that was made of iron called Moloch. People worshipping him would build a fire inside this god and heat the iron until it was red hot. They would sacrifice their baby or child by laying it on the arms of this god.

Really, nothing has changed since those days. People around the world still worship man-made images and animals, such as cows, rats, and crocodiles. They even worship certain men - some long dead - their bones lying in a tomb or grave somewhere. This is the result of people who knew the true and living God, but turned away into the awful world of false religion.

Chapter 6

The Origin of Sin

So, people have been sinning for a long time, but the original sin took place in heaven before man was even created. Gen 1:2 states, "The earth was formless and void, and darkness was over the surface of the deep, and the Spirit of God was moving over the surface of the waters." Why was the earth described in this way -- dark, shapeless, and covered with water? Why was the Spirit of God hovering (or on guard) over this formless void? Was it created this way? I use the Bible itself to explain portions of the scripture that are confusing due to lack of information. A possible answer to this question can be found in other parts of the Bible. The best way to interpret scripture is to find verses that are talking about the same subject. Again, please remember that the Bible is absolute truth. Please pray for understanding as you read its words.

The Bible says in Job 38:4-7, "Where were you when I laid the foundation of the earth? Tell Me, if you have understanding, Who set its measurements? Since you know. Or who stretched the line on it? On what were its bases sunk? Or who laid its cornerstone, When the morning stars sang together and all the sons of God shouted for joy?" Most Bible commentators feel that "morning stars" and "sons of God" refer to angels who serve and worship the God of creation. Would angels or sons of God have sung or shouted for joy over all that is described in verse 2 of Genesis 1 – the formlessness, the void, and the overpowering darkness?

God created all of the angels sometime before He made the earth. One of the angels is named Satan. When reading the Scriptures, he seems to be the most powerful and wisest of angels; he was given a high and lofty position in Heaven. In Ezekiel 28, music seemed to somehow be a part of him, and it sounded out to honor God. But (and there is most always a 'but'), there came a time when Satan convinced a third of the angels to attack the very throne of God with him. We are given an account of this in Isaiah 14:12-14:

"How you have fallen from heaven,
O star of the morning, son of the dawn!
You have been cut down to the earth,
You who have weakened the nations!
"But you said in your heart,
'I will ascend to heaven;
I will raise my throne above the stars of God,
And I will sit on the mount of assembly
In the recesses of the north.
'I will ascend above the heights of the clouds;
I will make myself like the Most High.'

Satan's rebellion was crushed by the archangel Michael and the other two thirds -- the loyal angels. As a result, Satan and his demons were cast to the earth. Jesus Himself saw it happen, "I was watching when I saw Satan cast like lightning to the earth." (Luke 10:18) (This event is also referenced in Ezekiel 28:11-16.) Judgment came on the earth, and this is likely why it became an awful place of loneliness and darkness, and why it was covered with water. Even right now there are angels who are imprisoned under water. Revelation 9:13,14 says, "Then the sixth angel sounded, and I heard a voice from the four horns of the golden alter which is before God, one saying to the sixth angel who had the trumpet. 'Release the four angels who are bound at the great river Euphrates.' And the four angels, who had been prepared for the hour and day and month and year, were released, so that they would kill a third of mankind." During the Persian Gulf War, as we watched scenes of fighting around the Euphrates River, I thought long and hard about these 4 angels being held prisoner somewhere in its depths.

When looking at the second part of Genesis 1:2, we then ask, "Why was the Spirit of God hovering over or guarding the earth?" I believe that He was holding Satan and his angels on this earth at that time. They were imprisoned until God chose to release them. How long they remained in this place -- we do not know.

In Proverbs 6:16-19, there is a list of things that God hates. Pride is at the top of the list. It is the main sin which drove Satan to rebel against God. Proverbs 16:5 says,

"Everyone who is proud in heart is an abomination to the Lord; Assuredly, he will not be unpunished." The Bible has a lot to say about pride and none of it is good. It is pride that is the driving force behind the theory of evolution. For example, a person may be more successful in the business world, and he looks down on people who have not done as well. He thinks it is because he has more ability than others. A person who is rightly related to God knows that the source of his success is from God and gives God the glory. He is more willing to share with those who are in need.

Chapter 7

Origin of Evening and Morning: Day 1

Genesis 1:3-5 states, "Then God said, 'Let there be light'; and there was light. God saw that the light was good; and God separated the light from the darkness. God called the light day, and the darkness He called night. And there was evening and there was morning, one day." (The Hebrew word for day is "yom" and means a 24-hour period.)

When God gave us the account of creation, there are a lot of details he did not tell us -- things that are a mystery to us. Again, how long was the earth dark and covered with water? Was the earth totally dark for 12 hours and totally light for 12 hours on this first day? Where did the light come from since there were no stars, sun, or moon? In answer to this last question, we do know that God Himself is the provider of light. We see this in Revelation 22:5: "And there will no longer be *any* night; and they will not have need of the light of a lamp nor the light of the sun, because the Lord God will illumine them; and they will reign forever and ever."

Day 1 was the first day in His plan to make this earth ready for the crown of His creation, mankind.

Chapter 8

Origin of Land and Water: Days 2 & 3

So, what happened on Day 2? Genesis 1:6-8 states, "Then God said, 'Let there be an expanse in the midst of the waters, and let it separate the waters from the waters.' God made the expanse, and separated the waters which were below the expanse from the waters which were above the expanse; and it was so. God called the expanse heaven. And there was evening and there was morning, a second day." On Day 2, God created the atmosphere.

Day 3 gives the origin of the great seas, plants, and fruit-bearing trees. God provided for vegetation by causing dry land to appear and the great seas to be separated into their own place. In this dry, fertile soil, He could then cause the plants to grow. Genesis 1:9-13 tells us, "Then God said, 'Let the waters below the heavens be gathered into one place, and let the dry land appear'; and it was so. God called the dry land earth, and the gathering of the waters He called seas; and God saw that it was good. Then God said, 'Let the earth sprout vegetation, plants yielding seed, *and* fruit trees on the earth bearing fruit after their kind with seed in them'; and it was so. The earth brought forth vegetation, plants yielding seed after their kind, and trees bearing fruit with seed in them, after their kind; and God saw that it was good. There was evening and there was morning, a third day."

Days 2 and 3 were the next days in His plan to make this earth ready for man. Man needs vegetables, fruits, and other plants to live healthy lives. God also provides some fascinating plant life for his viewing pleasure. When man appears on the earth, he will find them waiting for him.

A "CREATION MOMENT":
COAT OF MANY COLORS

Genesis 37:3

"Now Israel loved Joseph more than all his children, because he was the son of his old age: and he made him a coat of many colours."

The rainbow eucalyptus tree is undoubtedly the most beautiful tree ever. Its bark looks like it was painted by an artist using a palette full of pastel pigments. Surprisingly, this tree's coat of many colors actually comes from the way its bark peels off the tree.

According to research botanist LariAnn Garner: "As the newly exposed bark slowly ages, it changes from bright green to a darker green, then bluish to purplish, and then pink-orange. Finally, the color becomes a brownish maroon right before exfoliation occurs." She also notes that "since this process is happening in different zones of the trunk and in different stages simultaneously, the colors are varied and almost constantly changing. As a result, the tree will never have the same color pattern twice, making it like a work of living art."

The rainbow eucalyptus is also among the fastest-growing trees. It begins as a seed smaller than an ant and grows as much as eight feet per year, eventually rising up to a height of a hundred feet. And here's a surprising fact. These rainbow-colored trees are used mainly to make white paper!

Though evolutionists attribute the tree's colors to natural selection, we must point out that there are many other kinds of trees with peeling bark — including several varieties of maple trees — but the bark of these trees do not undergo a color transformation like this. Evolution had nothing to do with it. These trees are, indeed, a living piece of art painted by their Creator!

Prayer:
Heavenly Father, no human artist can come close to achieving the beauty I see in Your creation! More beautiful than Your creation, however, is Your glorious plan of salvation! Amen.

Notes:

L. Garner, "Under the Rainbow", Ornamental Outlook, 9/06. This website features many photos of the rainbow eucalyptus tree:

http://www.lovethesepics.com/2013/01/living-rainbow-rainbow-eucalyptus-most-beautiful-tree-bark-on-earth-36-pics/. Photo: Rainbow eucalyptus trees. Courtesy of Amelia. (CC-BY-SA 2.0)

Chapter 9

Origin of the Sun, Moon, and Stars: Day 4

Genesis 1:14-19 states, "Then God said, 'Let there be lights in the expanse of the heavens to separate the day from the night, and let them be for signs and for seasons and for days and years; and let them be for lights in the expanse of the heavens to give light on the earth'; and it was so. God made the two great lights, the greater light to govern the day, and the lesser light to govern the night; *He made* the stars also. God placed them in the expanse of the heavens to give light on the earth, and to govern the day and the night, and to separate the light from the darkness; and God saw that it was good. There was evening and there was morning, a fourth day."

Here God created the sun, the greater light, and the moon, the lesser light. The earth spins around on its axis taking 24 hours to make a complete rotation. This gives us one day. The moon has its own orbit around the earth which takes about 29 days. This rotation gives us one month. As the earth spins, it is also revolving in its orbit around the sun taking 1 year or about 365 days for one revolution. We need the sun's light during the day and, at night, we need the lesser light from the moon and stars.

Consider what is happening around us as we walk, breathe, and live our lives. We often take it for granted because all creation is working together in perfect harmony. Let's consider 3 facts: The first fact is that our earth is nearly 93 million miles from the sun. It is perfectly located. Any closer and we could not live as it would be too hot; any further away and we would freeze. Secondly, the moon serves not only as light but also as a control over the oceans' tides. If the moon did not exert a certain amount of gravitational pull in its orbit around the earth, the seas would overflow the land. Finally, the earth is traveling in its orbit about 1,000 miles per hour in perfect balance. What happens if you are carrying a bowl full of water and the bowl tilts or if your speed of walking changes? The water in the bowl tends to splash out. What if the earth should suddenly slow down for instance or speed up? We know, though, that none of these things will happen because our God is always in control. He never has to stop or rest. He is faithfully keeping everything under control.

The end of Genesis 1:16 says: "He made the stars also." This phrase of five words seems to have been written as an afterthought. Let's stop and absorb just what is involved in this tiny statement. Astronomers say that there are more stars in the heavens than all the grains of sand on all the beaches on the earth. (I heard Deputy Barney Fife say this, too, on one of the Andy Griffith shows, so it's a fact.) How far is it from our star – the sun - to our next neighbor star? The late Dr. Irwin Moon and Moody Bible

Institute's Science Department made some wonderful and informative videos for children, youth, and adults. In the film *God of Creation*, he gives us this insight:

If we leave the sun at 12:00 p.m. on January 1, traveling 186,000 miles per second, we would pass Mercury and Venus and reach earth in 8 minutes and 19 seconds. Continuing on, at 5:31 that evening, we would pass Pluto, having traveled 3 billion 675 million miles, and it is still January 1! On April 19 (Yep.) --- 5 years later (Really?), we would reach the nearest star, Alpha Centauri. There are 100 million stars in known space which is only 1 billionth of our known universe. How many stars are there? Scientists say the number would be 100 billion X 100 million X 1,000 million which equals 10  octillion (10,000,000,000,000,000,000,000,000,000) or 10^{28}. That IS about equal to all the grains of sand on all the seashores of the world.

On one day, God created all of this. Psalm 8:5 says we have seen only the work of God's fingers

Carl Sagan, a leading evolution scientist, died in 1996. Just before his death, he was interviewed by Ted Koppel on the TV show *Nightline*. Koppel asked him, "Dr. Sagan, do you have any pearls of wisdom that you would like to give to the human race?" Sagan replied, "We live on a hunk of rock and metal that circles a humdrum star that is one of 400 billion other stars that make up the Milky Way Galaxy, which is one of billions of other galaxies, which make up a universe, which may be one of a very large number--perhaps an infinite number--of other universes. That is a perspective on human life and our culture that is well worth pondering."

On day 4 God created all the galaxies. Psalm 147:4 says, "He counts the number of stars; He gives names to all of them." Isaiah 40:26 gives encouragement: "Lift up your eyes on high and see who has created these stars, the One who leads forth their host by number. He calls them all by name. Because of the greatness of His might and the strength of his power not one of them is missing."

A "CREATION MOMENT":
THE SUN, MOON, AND STARS

Psalm 8:3-4
"When I consider thy heavens, the work of thy fingers, the moon and the stars, which thou hast ordained; What is man, that thou art mindful of him? And the son of man, that thou visitest him?"

What is the most awesome show of God's power? It may not be what you think.

Origins: The Road to the Messiah

In Psalm 8:3 4, the psalmist is led to exclaim, "When I consider Your heavens, the work of Your fingers, the moon and stars which you have ordained, what is man that You are mindful of him…?" If the night sky is a glory we can only stare at in awe, our telescopes and space probes have shown us that we can see very little of its true glory.

Consider our sun. Less than 0.10 percent of all the sun's energy falls on the Earth. Yet if just that small fraction of power could be harnessed, we would never have any energy shortage. But we have learned that our sun is only an average sized star in our galaxy of over 1 billion stars! We have no way to even measure that kind of energy! Even more awesome is that our galaxy is only one of more than a million galaxies! What is a billion times immeasurable energy? And God made and energized it all in just one day!

As hard as all of this is to understand, what is even harder for us to comprehend about God's working is that all of this was created through the power of God's Word – that same Word that became flesh and dwelt among us! Truly, His love for us is beyond our comprehension!

Photo: Extreme Deep Field photo taken by the Hubble space telescope. Each speck is a galaxy. Courtesy of NASA.

Chapter 10

Theistic Evolution

Theistic evolution is a theory which states that the God who made the heavens and the earth is not personally involved in his creation. He created the building blocks and the natural laws that exist, and now, He just sits back and watches the world go round. He is not concerned with what happens to each of us as individuals or even animals and plants.

I do not know what god they are talking about, but it is not the God of the Bible. Hebrews 1:1-4 says, "God after he spoke long ago to the fathers in the prophets in many portions and in many ways, in these last days has spoken to us in the Son, whom He appointed heir of all things, through whom He also made the world. And He is the radiance of his glory and the exact representation of His nature, and upholds all things by the word of His power."

Psalm 104 declares that God is totally involved in feeding and caring for all the things he has created. In this psalm, God is taking care of the earth as a whole, the seas, the animals, the birds, and man himself. He controls the moon for the seasons and keeps the great ocean tides in check. The great seas which swarm with fish, even

Leviathan (What a creature! Read more about him in Job 41.), wait for God to give them their food. All 35 verses of this chapter give praise to the God of creation and depend on his faithfulness to provide what they need:

"The Lord's Care over All His Works
Bless the Lord, O my soul!
O Lord my God, You are very great;
You are clothed with splendor and majesty,
Covering Yourself with light as with a cloak,
Stretching out heaven like a *tent* curtain.
He lays the beams of His upper chambers in the waters;
He makes the clouds His chariot;
He walks upon the wings of the wind;
He makes the winds His messengers,
Flaming fire His ministers.
He established the earth upon its foundations,
So that it will not totter forever and ever.
You covered it with the deep as with a garment;
The waters were standing above the mountains.
At Your rebuke they fled,
At the sound of Your thunder they hurried away.
The mountains rose; the valleys sank down
To the place which You established for them.
You set a boundary that they may not pass over,
So that they will not return to cover the earth.
He sends forth springs in the valleys;
They flow between the mountains;
They give drink to every beast of the field;
The wild donkeys quench their thirst.
Beside them the birds of the heavens dwell;

Origins: The Road to the Messiah

They lift up *their* voices among the branches.
He waters the mountains from His upper chambers;
The earth is satisfied with the fruit of His works.
He causes the grass to grow for the cattle,
And vegetation for the labor of man,
So that he may bring forth food from the earth,
And wine which makes man's heart glad,
So that he may make *his* face glisten with oil,
And food which sustains man's heart.
The trees of the Lord drink their fill,
The cedars of Lebanon which He planted,
Where the birds build their nests,
And the stork, whose home is the fir trees.
The high mountains are for the wild goats;
The cliffs are a refuge for the shephanim.

He made the moon for the seasons;
The sun knows the place of its setting.
You appoint darkness and it becomes night,
In which all the beasts of the forest prowl about.
The young lions roar after their prey
And seek their food from God.
When the sun rises they withdraw
And lie down in their dens.
Man goes forth to his work
And to his labor until evening.

O Lord, how many are Your works!
In wisdom You have made them all;
The earth is full of Your possessions.
There is the sea, great and broad,

In which are swarms without number,
Animals both small and great.
There the ships move along,
And Leviathan, which You have formed to sport in it.
They all wait for You
To give them their food in due season.
You give to them, they gather *it* up;
You open Your hand, they are satisfied with good.
You hide Your face, they are dismayed;
You take away their spirit, they expire
And return to their dust.
You send forth Your Spirit, they are created;
And You renew the face of the ground.
Let the glory of the Lord endure forever;
Let the Lord be glad in His works;
He looks at the earth, and it trembles;
He touches the mountains, and they smoke.
I will sing to the Lord as long as I live;
I will sing praise to my God while I have my being.
Let my meditation be pleasing to Him;
As for me, I shall be glad in the Lord.
Let sinners be consumed from the earth
And let the wicked be no more.
Bless the Lord, O my soul.
Praise the Lord!"

Chapter 11

Days 5 and 6:
Fish, Birds, Insects, and Animals

On Day 5, God created the water creatures and birds. According to Genesis 1:20, 21, "God said, "Let the waters teem with swarms of living creatures and let birds fly above the earth in the open expanse of the heavens. God created the great sea monsters and every living creature that moves with which the waters swarmed after their kind, and every winged bird after its kind; and God saw that it was good."

Verse 22 states that "God blessed them, saying 'Be fruitful and multiply, and fill the waters in the seas, and let birds multiply on the earth'." Verse 23 concludes by saying, "There was evening and morning, the fifth day."

Verses 24 and 25 give the origin of the land animals: "Then God said, 'Let the earth bring forth living creatures after their kind: cattle and creeping things and beasts of the earth after their kind'; and it was so. God made the beasts of the earth after their kind, and the cattle after their kind, and everything that creeps on the ground after its kind; and God saw that it was good." God made the beasts of the earth after their kind -- or species. These would be non-domesticated animals, animals not designed for doing work for man. These may bears, lions, porcupines, or ticks. I think He got a little creative when He made the aye aye, the pink fairy armadillo, the star-nosed mole, and the naked mole rat – look them up online to see how odd they are. Also, He made the cattle after their kind -- or species. Animals such as cows, horses, oxen, donkeys, and Chihuahuas were domesticated; they could be used for the service of man.

Animals cannot reproduce outside their own species. For instance, a bird cannot produce a cat, or a dog cannot produce a tiger. In 1 Corinthians 15:39, Paul says, "All flesh is not the same flesh, but there is one flesh of men, and another flesh of beasts, and another flesh of birds, and another of fish." Animals are made up of various combinations of amino acids. A dog is made of the combination that makes it a dog. A superb bird of paradise has its own combination; a blob fish has its own combination. According to Dr. John MacArthur's book *Battle for the Beginning*, there are over 640 octillion decillion combinations of amino acids, the building blocks of all living things. This lone fact helps debunk Charles Darwin's theory that animals can evolve from one species to another.

And, finally, notice the end of Genesis 1:25. It states, "And God saw that it was good."

The world is now ready for the crown of God's creation:
mankind.

A "CREATION MOMENT"
THE WORLD'S UGLIEST ANIMAL?

Romans 5:8
"But God commendeth his love toward us, in that, while
we were yet sinners, Christ died for us."

When this fish is taken out of the water, its face almost looks like a very sad person. In 2013 it was voted the "World's Ugliest Animal". What is this creature that was adopted as the mascot of the Ugly Animal Preservation Society? It's the appropriately named blobfish.

Photos of the ugly blobfish have been making the  rounds on the Internet. And yet, even the blobfish has beauty when you consider that it was designed to function perfectly in its environment.

Blobfish inhabit the deep waters off the coasts of Australia, Tasmania and New Zealand. If you wanted to see one in its natural habitat, you would have to dive to a depth of between 2,000 and 3,900 feet where the pressure is several dozen times higher than at sea level. The pressure is no problem for the blobfish, though. Its jelly-like body is slightly less dense than water, allowing it to float effortlessly just above the sea floor.

Blobfish don't have much muscle for swimming, but they don't need it. They simply swallow edible matter that floats into their mouth. Sadly, they are an endangered species because of fishing trawlers dragging their nets on the seafloor.

Yes, the blobfish is far from attractive. But it serves as a reminder that sinful human beings are unattractive in the sight of God. And yet, while we were still sinners, God sent His Son to die for us and to exchange His righteousness for our sins, making us acceptable in God's sight. What a Savior!

Prayer:
Father, thank You for sending Your Holy Spirit to reveal the ugliness brought about by sin. Thank You also for sending Your Son to remove my sin and make me righteous in Your sight. Amen.

Notes:

"So you think you've had a bad day? Spare a thought for the world's most miserable-looking fish, which is now in danger of being wiped out," Mail Online, 1-26-10. http://www.dailymail.co.uk/news/article.1245955/Worlds -miserable-looking-fish-danger-wiped out.html#ixzz38i3nZRZK.

Photo: Blobfish. Courtesy of Kids Discover Magazine.https://www.facebook.com/kidsdiscover/photo s/pb.157635677358.2207520000.1407342467./10152612 378327359/?type=1&theater.

Chapter 12

Origin of Man and Woman
and Satan's Lie: Day 6

Gen 1:26, 27 states, "Then God said, 'Let Us make man in Our image, according to Our likeness; and let them rule over the fish of the sea and over the birds of the sky and over the cattle and over all the earth, and over every creeping thing that creeps on the earth.' God created man in His own image, in the image of God He created him; male and female He created them. So God created man in his own image, in the image of God he created him, male and female he created them." Day 6 describes the origin of mankind. The very first person God created was a man, and God gave him a name, Adam. God gave Adam the privilege of naming all the animals. God would bring an animal to Adam, and Adam would give it a name and whatever Adam called it, that was its name. Wouldn't that be fun? Names are important to God. Anywhere you go in this world, people have personal names. I guess every person who has ever lived has been called something. God knows every star that He created and knows each one of them by name. That is amazing because, as we discussed earlier, there are more stars in the universe than all the grains of sand on all the beaches in the world.

God made sure that all the living creatures had his own mate, but for Adam there was not a mate, or helper, suitable for Him. Gen 2:21-25 states, "So the Lord God caused a deep sleep to fall upon the man, and he slept; then He took one of his ribs and closed up the flesh at that place. The Lord God fashioned into a woman the rib which He had taken from the man, and brought her to the man. The man said, 'This is now bone of my bones, And flesh of my flesh; She shall be called Woman, Because she was taken out of Man'. For this reason a man shall leave his father and his mother, and be joined to his wife; and they shall become one flesh. And the man and his wife were both naked and were not ashamed." This here was the origin of the first marriage. Every human being that has ever been born would descend from these two. Right in the face of his most bitter enemy, Satan, God placed man who had been created in God's own image. Imagine what it has been like for Satan. Every time he sees a human being, it stirs up a murderous rage. You know why there is so much pain, suffering, lying, hatred and murder in the human race? It all originated from Satan, who Jesus identified as being the father of liars and murderers. John 8:44 states, "You are of your father the devil, and you want to do the desires of your father. He was a murderer from the beginning, and does not stand in the truth because there is no truth in him. Whenever he speaks a lie, he speaks from his own nature, for he is a liar and the father of lies."

Satan tried in vain to overthrow God and be God and to be worshipped as God. Now, Satan has two main objectives. First, he still wants to be worshipped, and second, he knows his ultimate destiny is the lake of fire and he wants to take as many men as he can with him. Let's use our brain to think about something important: God had given Adam and Eve dominion over the earth. All the animals were subject unto them. The couple was given a beautiful place to live, the Garden of Eden. Genesis 2:9 and 15-17 describe it, "Out of the ground the Lord God caused to grow every tree that is pleasing to the sight and good for food; the tree of life also in the midst of the garden, and the tree of the knowledge of good and evil. Then the Lord God took the man and put him into the Garden of Eden to cultivate it and keep it. The Lord God commanded the man, saying, 'From any tree of the garden you may eat freely; but from the tree of the knowledge of good and evil you shall not eat, for in the day that you eat from it you will surely die'." Why did God put this condition upon man? Well, God created man to have someone with whom he could have fellowship. Before the Fall, Adam and Eve were at perfect harmony with God. Both could stand in the very presence of God without fear or shame. They could communicate back and forth in a personal way as we can with each other today. God created man to worship God. True worship involves a personal willingness to do so. True worship of God requires that man take God at His word when he speaks. In order to have a free will to worship and communicate with God, there has to be in place a chance to prove himself by an act or acts of obedience. Adam and Eve had only this one thing to obey. Simply put, do not eat of this particular tree. Nothing hard at all, nothing complicated. Eat of this tree and surely die or do not eat and surely live. To live in this case was to continue his perfect harmony and fellowship with God. Everything had started out so good for mankind.

There was no death; animals did not eat each another; there were no thorns or kudzu, NO spiders or poisonous snakes! No mosquitoes that bite, no pesky flies, no toxic plants, no worm-eaten fruit. Labor was not tiresome, but totally enjoyable. Adam and Eve did not suffer from any kind of illness or disease. They did not suffer from being too cold or too hot. Best of all, they were in perfect fellowship with their Creator.

Chapter 13

Man's Fall

Sadly, this perfect environment did not last as Adam and Eve eventually ate of the forbidden fruit. This event sent mankind into a downward spiral, breaking the fellowship they had with God. They were sent out of the garden into a world where a curse had come. They would now have to labor for food and suffer terribly when giving birth. As warned, they suffered spiritual death immediately and would one day suffer physical death.

Let's look at what happened in detail. Genesis 3:1-7 says, "Now the serpent was more crafty than any beast of the field which the Lord God had made. And he said to the woman, 'Indeed, has God said, "You shall not eat from any tree of the garden"?' The woman said to the serpent, 'From the fruit of the trees of the garden we may eat; but from the fruit of the tree which is in the middle of the garden, God has said, "You shall not eat from it or touch it, or you will die."' The serpent said to the woman, 'You surely will not die! For God knows that in the day you eat from it your eyes will be opened, and you will be like God, knowing good and evil.' When the woman saw that the tree was good for food, and that it was a delight to the eyes, and that the tree was desirable to make *one* wise, she took from its fruit and ate; and she gave also to her husband with her, and he ate. Then the eyes of both of them were opened, and they knew that they were naked; and they sewed fig leaves together and made themselves loin coverings."

Note Satan's opening in the form of a question: "Has God said, 'You shall not eat from any tree of the garden'?" Let me put this into an illustration. Suppose you have been given some important information - maybe some instruction from your parents or your boss. Immediately afterward, someone else comes along, and like Satan, has an evil intent. He or she wants to make you disobey. They knows what you have been told. They come on like this, "Did your dad really tell you...?" (And they quote from your dad's own words). You answer, "Yes, he said ...." Well, this sly, evil-intentioned person says, "I was afraid of that. Good thing I came along to straighten you out."

Satan is very good at this. It worked on Eve, and she was in the *BEST* possible conditions – a perfect environment with a perfect body. But in hers and Adam's being was the ability to use their brains, to choose, the ability to think things over, to evaluate the conflicting information given to them first by God, then by Satan. Sadly, Eve gave in to the temptation. She answered the serpent by misquoting God, "You shall not eat or touch it." God never said they could not touch it, never gave them any instruction, except not to eat of it. That is all. So simple. But now that she has misquoted God, Satan follows up with his own responses: "You surely will not die" and "If you listen to me your eyes will be opened and you will be like God." Satan hit Eve on three fronts: her eyes lusted, his reasoning got into her mind and made her doubt God, and his lies appealed to her hearing.

Four thousand years or so later, Satan tried to cause Jesus to fall using this same method. Jesus was driven by the Spirit into the wilderness, the *WORST* possible environment, and went without food for 40 days. He was also all alone. (See Matthew chapter 4 for the account.) Jesus stood the tests Satan threw at him. He did not yield to Satan's temptations.

After Adam and Eve had both eaten of the forbidden fruit, their eyes were immediately opened. Their innocence was gone. They both realized they were naked and tried to cover themselves with fig leaves.

The moment they disobeyed God, they experienced spiritual death. The position they had had with God, that perfect harmony, communication, and fellowship was broken. Here is the narrative of what happened in Genesis 3:8-15: "They heard the sound of the Lord God walking in the garden in the cool of the day, and the man and his wife hid themselves from the presence of the Lord God among the trees of the garden. Then the Lord God called to the man, and said to him, 'Where are you?' He said, 'I heard the sound of You in the garden, and I was afraid because I was naked; so I hid myself.' And He said, 'Who told you that you were naked? Have you eaten from the tree of which I commanded you not to eat?' The man said, 'The woman whom You gave *to be* with me, she gave me from the tree, and I ate.' Then the Lord God said to the woman, 'What is

this you have done?' And the woman said, 'The serpent deceived me, and I ate.' The Lord God said to the serpent, 'Because you have done this,
Cursed are you more than all cattle,
And more than every beast of the field;
On your belly you will go,
And dust you will eat
All the days of your life;
 And I will put enmity
Between you and the woman,
And between your seed and her seed;
He shall bruise you on the head,
And you shall bruise him on the heel."

A "CREATION MOMENT": GOD'S UNUSUAL FIG ARRANGEMENT

Habakkuk 3:17-18
"Although the fig tree shall not blossom, neither shall fruit be in the vines; the labour of the olive shall fail, and the fields shall yield no meat; the flock shall be cut off from the fold, and there shall be no herd in the stalls: yet I will rejoice in the LORD, I will joy in the God of my salvation."

Completely unrelated creatures that depend entirely upon one another to live and have no way of living without one another pose a very serious challenge to those who claim that all living things evolved. The relationship is called reciprocal altruism.

One startling example is the relationship between the fig wasp and the fig tree. Male figs are not for eating; they produce the pollen to pollinate the sweet, juicy female fig. But the flower parts of both the male and female figs are inside the figs. There is no chance that the wind could spread pollen from the male to the female figs. And there is no other creature except the fig wasp that can transfer the pollen.

Herein lies an incredible story. The fig wasp hatches from eggs inside the male fig, and its purpose in its short 24-hour life is to lay its eggs inside another male fig. The female wasp emerges from the male fig covered in pollen and is programmed 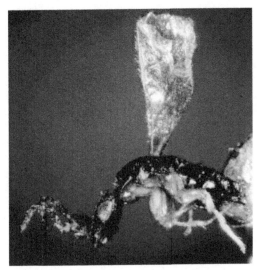 to search among the female figs, thus fertilizing them, before laying its eggs inside a male fig and, thus, starting the cycle again.

The fig wasp will only lay its eggs in the male fig while the female fig cannot be pollinated by any other method. Clearly, both the fig wasp and the fig tree were created for this special relationship.

Prayer:

Dear Lord, just as You created the fig wasp and the fig tree for this close relationship, You have created me for a relationship with You. There is no peace for me outside of a relationship with You. Help me to grow closer to You through the instruction of Your Word. Amen.

Notes:

Photo: Pollinating fig wasp. Courtesy of Anthony Bain. (CC-BY-SA 3.0)

Chapter 14

A Covering for Man
and the Wickedness of Man

The Road to the Messiah begins here. It is an awful, bloody road filled with pain, suffering, and death.

After receiving their punishments from God, Adam's and Eve's Creator "made garments of skin" and clothed them. An animal (or animals) had to give its life for them to have a covering to hide their nakedness. Jesus Christ would one day give up his life so we could have our sins covered, so that we can stand in the presence of a holy God without shame.

Through the entirety of the Old Testament, God is working to keep the lineage to the Messiah secure. A lineage is a direct line of descent from one ancestor to the next. The Messiah was first mentioned as "her seed" in Genesis 3:13b-15:

"And the woman said, 'The serpent deceived me, and I ate.'
The Lord God said to the serpent,
'Because you have done this,
Cursed are you more than all cattle,
And more than every beast of the field;
On your belly you will go,
And dust you will eat
All the days of your life;
And I will put enmity
Between you and the woman,
And between your seed and **her seed**;
He shall bruise you on the head,
And you shall bruise him on the heel."

Satan reacted to God's announcement of His Messiah with an evil plan of his own. He would set up a world filled with people so wicked, that there would be no one through whom God could fulfill this promise. Jeremiah 17:9, "The heart is more deceitful than all else and is desperately sick; Who can understand it?" Genesis 6:5, "Then the Lord saw that the wickedness of man was great on the earth, and that every intent of the thoughts of his heart was only evil continually." The heart of man is by nature full of evil. I once spoke with a man who did not believe this. He was sure that he could make it to heaven on his own merit. I asked him if all the thoughts of his heart, all his motives, all the things he had done, whether good or bad, were put up on a movie screen, what would the Motion Picture Association of America rate it? Would it be fit for children to watch? How would it compare to the most violent or pornographic movie Hollywood has ever made?

He could not answer truthfully, so he dodged my question.

The thing Satan does, and is very good at it, is create an environment where evil can flourish. In Genesis 6:1-4 it states, "Now it came about, when men began to multiply on the face of the land, and daughters were born to them, that the sons of God saw that the daughters of men were beautiful; and they took wives for themselves, whomever they chose. Then the Lord said, 'My Spirit shall not strive with man forever, because he also is flesh; nevertheless his days shall be one hundred and twenty years.' The Nephilim were on the earth in those days, and also afterward, when the sons of God came in to the daughters of men, and they bore *children* to them. Those were the mighty men who *were* of old, men of renown." There is a difference of opinion as to what or who the "sons of God" were who are mentioned in verse 2. Some say the "sons of God" refer to the godly line of Seth, the son given to Adam and Eve after Cain killed Abel. They say that fallen angels could never be called the "sons of God." The other view is the one I hold to. This view sees the sons of God *as* fallen angels. The book of Job 1:6 states, "Now there was a day when the sons of God came to present themselves before the Lord, and Satan also came among them." This is reiterated in Job 2:1: "Again there was a day when the sons of God came to present themselves before the Lord, and Satan also came among them to present himself before the Lord."

Sometimes fallen angels are called "angels," and not always "demons." This view sees the "sons of God" possessing men which reproduced with women of the earth leading to the "mighty men who *were* of old, men of renown" in verse 4. Remember, in Revelation 9:13-15 it says, "Then the sixth angel sounded, and I heard a voice from the four horns of the golden altar which is before God, One saying to the sixth angel who had the trumpet, 'Release the 4 angels who are bound at the great river Euphrates.' And the four angels, who had been prepared for the hour and day and month and year, were released, so that they would kill a third of mankind." Some fallen angels were so wicked that they were no longer allowed to roam the Earth. Jude 6 gives us more insight about what happened: "And angels who did not keep their own domain, but abandoned their proper abode, He has kept in eternal bonds under darkness for the judgment of the great day." Could these two instances of angel punishment be the result of what happened in Genesis 6? Could these fallen angels have committed sins so grievous that God destroyed all the inhabitants of the earth with the flood? In back of it all was Satan's attempt to corrupt mankind so that there would be no Messiah to come and fulfill the promise He made in Genesis 3:15.

For six thousand years or so, the whole earth itself has been groaning under the curse. Adam and Eve experienced its awful ramifications when their oldest son Cain murdered his brother in a fit of jealous range.

Romans chapter 8 verses 20 -23, For the creation was subjected to futility, not willingly, but because of Him who subjected it, but in hope that the creation itself also will be set free from its slavery to corruption into the freedom of the glory of the children of God For we know that the whole creation groans and suffers the pains of childbirth until now.

Chapter 15

Noah Building The Ark
And The Great Flood

As the population grew, the people too grew – grew so desperately wicked that God had to judge the earth. He did it by flooding the whole earth with water, drowning the people and animals on the earth. The only ones who escaped were a man named Noah, his wife, and their three sons (Shem, Ham, and Japheth) and their wives. Noah built an ark according to the instructions God had given him. For 120 years, he worked on the ark, all the while preaching to the people that judgment was coming in the form of a great flood. Second Peter 2:4,5 says, "For if God did not spare angels when they sinned, but cast them into hell and committed them to pits of darkness, reserved for judgment; and did not spare the ancient world, but preserved Noah, a preacher of righteousness, with seven others, when He brought a flood upon the world of the ungodly..." And, for 120 years as Noah (and hopefully his crew of carpenters) built, the people scoffed and made fun -- after all, it had never rained, so they carried on with their wicked ways.

One wonderful day the people saw a strange sight. Animals and birds of all kinds were filing and flying into the ark. Noah and his family got on board, and God Himself shut the door -- the Only Door. For 7 days nothing happened. Then the skies opened up and down came a massive torrent of rain. The water that was under the ground came spewing up out of the deep. This kept up for 40 days and 40 nights, drowning all the people and land animals. But God remembered Noah, his family, and all the animals that were on the ark. God stopped the rain from the sky and stopped up the fountains of the deep. God caused a wind to pass over the earth and the water began to subside.

The ark came to rest on Mount Ararat in modern day Turkey. The water decreased steadily, and soon the tops of the mountains appeared. Forty days later, Noah opened the window of the ark and let out a raven. The raven never returned to the ark so Noah sent out a dove which did come back to the ark. Noah waited 7 more days and sent out the dove again which returned with an olive leaf in her beak. He waited 7 additional days and sent out the dove which did not return.

Why did the raven not return to the ark? It was because the raven found a feast outside. There were stinking dead bodies of people and animals floating and laying around. The nature of a raven is to feed on dead, rotting flesh. A person who has not been born again by the Spirit likes to feed on the dead things of this world. He or she loves the deeds of the flesh like immorality, impurity, sensuality, idolatry, sorcery, enmities, strife, jealousy, anger, dissensions, factions, envying, drunkenness, and carousing. These are found in Galatians 5:19-21.

The dove has a nature that does not care for dead, rotting flesh. It looks for clean things such as berries, seeds, or fruit. A person who belongs to God has a new nature that enjoys the things of God. Galatians 5:22–24 states, "But the fruit of the Spirit is love, joy, peace, patience, kindness, goodness, faithfulness, gentleness, self-control; against such things there is no law. Now those who belong to Christ Jesus have crucified the flesh with its passions and desires."

A Couple of Really Interesting Facts

1. Methuselah was the son of Enoch and the grandfather of Noah. He died in the year 1656 at the ripe old age of 969. His name means "When he dies, it will come" referring to the flood in Noah's day. He lived longer than any man that had ever lived, and He died 7 days before the rain began.

2. God told Noah to cover the ark with pitch. The Hebrew word for pitch is "kopher," a waterproof covering. No matter how bad the storm was raging outside the ark, the pitch kept the occupants inside safe and dry. The word "atonement" appears several times in the Old Testament. The Hebrew word is "kophar," which also means a covering. The blood of bulls and goats never took away the penalty for sin, but pointed to the Lamb of God, our Messiah, who

would permanently take away sin. First John 1:7b states, "The blood of Jesus His Son cleanses us from all sin."

Chapter 16

After The Flood Waters Dried Up

The day came when God told Noah that it was time to leave the ark. The land was dry and the world was ready to be repopulated. So, Noah and his wife, his 3 sons, and 3 daughters-in-law left the ark and moved into a new world. The animals, with their mates, left the ark and journeyed out to repopulate the earth.

The first thing Noah did was to build an altar to the Lord. He took of every clean animal and clean bird and offered burnt offerings unto the Lord. Remember that back Genesis 7:2, Noah was told to take 7 of each clean animal and bird for making sacrifices. When the Lord smelled the aroma, He was pleased and vowed to Himself that he would never again destroy everything as He had just done.

Remember too, in Genesis 1:14, God made lights in the heavens to "separate the day from the night, and let them be for signs and for seasons and for days and years." Right after Noah left the ark and offered his sacrifices, God reaffirmed that the 4 seasons and day and night would continue:

"While the earth remains,
Seedtime and harvest,
And cold and heat,
And summer and winter,
And day and night
Shall not cease."

God also made changes to man's diet. Before the flood, people were vegetarians. Genesis 9:3-5 states, "Every moving thing that is alive shall be food for you; I give all to you, as *I gave* the green plant. Only you shall not eat flesh with its life, *that is*, its blood. Surely I will require your lifeblood; from every beast I will require it. And from *every* man, from every man's brother I will require the life of man." So, from that day forward, mankind could feast on filet mignon, escargot, bologna, and deer jerky, along with his spinach salad and salsa with chips.

Today there are religious organizations which believe in eating only plant matter in their religious ceremonies. J. Vernon McGee of *Through the Bible Radio* was discussing this with a woman who headed up a group of people who practiced this quest for spirituality. He reminded her that it was a whole world of vegetarians that God drowned in the flood.

There are also organizations that would put a stop to the killing and eating of animals. They say that there is no difference between killing animals and killing people. The founder of PETA (People for the Ethical Treatment of

Animals), Ingrid Newkirk, began this organization with this motto: "When it comes to pain, love, joy, loneliness, and fear, a rat is a pig is a dog is a boy. Each one values his or her life and fights the knife." This motto sounds pretty good, but on their website today, the main heading proclaims, "Animals are NOT ours to eat, wear, experiment on, use for entertainment, or abuse in any other way." Man is created in the image of God; animals are not. Animals do not have a soul that will live forever like man does. When an animal dies, its body goes back to the earth never to live again. After the flood, God changed man's diet and made it okay to consume animal meat.

There are groups that would have all hunting stopped. If that were to happen, it would bring about such an overpopulation of animals that there would not be enough food to sustain them. Consider this fact from Penn State: "In 1900 there were estimated to be only 500,000 white tailed deer in the continental United States. Today, however, this population is estimated to be over 15,000,000 individuals!" Also, the eating of wild animals such as deer, rabbits or squirrels is very good for our health. The meat is low-fat and lacks preservatives and steroids often found in the meat purchased from local grocery stores. Native Americans had to depend on killing animals for food, clothing, and shelter. When settlers came to this country and built their homes, they could not have survived on a vegetable diet only. It would have been the same for the sons of Noah as they moved out to build their homes and families.

Vegetation had been devastated by the flood and would have to regenerate. I can imagine that fresh fish would have been easy to get at first as they would have been trapped in pools of water.

I do know people who are vegetarians by their own choice; that is perfectly okay and I do not think they should be faulted. The Apostle Paul gave us some important instructions in Romans 14: "Now accept the one who is weak in faith, *but* not for *the purpose of* passing judgment on his opinions. One person has faith that he may eat all things, but he who is weak eats vegetables *only*. The one who eats is not to regard with contempt the one who does not eat, and the one who does not eat is not to judge the one who eats, for God has accepted him. Paul also encourages us by saying, "Whether, then, you eat or drink or whatever you do, do all to the glory of God." (1 Corinthians10:31)

My point in all of this is that God ordained the killing and eating of animals. The organizations that teach otherwise are simply misinformed about what God has said. In the Old Testament, under Judaic law, sheep, lambs, goats, oxen, and doves were offered as sacrifices by the millions, all under God's authority. The priests offering them were allowed to eat most of the meat. These sacrifices pointed to the coming of Jesus, our Messiah, who would shed his own blood on the cross paying our sin debt, thus putting an end to animal sacrifices.

It is fine to enjoy eating meat, but no one should ever mistreat animals, causing them pain and suffering. In the middle of winter, I once came upon two little puppies that somebody had set off out where there were no houses for miles. It was one of the saddest sights I have ever seen. One pup was making the most pitiful wailing sound I have ever heard. His little buddy was already dead and the live puppy was cuddled up against it. I brought the living puppy home and fed it but it only lived a couple of days. What a cold hearted, evil thing somebody had done. Jesus said that His Father in heaven sees when a sparrow falls to the ground, so He was watching whoever committed this deed. There will come a day when he or she will face the Judge of all the earth. Proverbs 12:10 says, "A righteous man has regard for the life of his animal, But even the compassions of the wicked is cruel."

Chapter 17

Origin of Languages

After leaving the ark, God gave instructions to Noah and his sons. He told them to move out across the whole earth and repopulate it. Instead, they chose to remain fairly close to home. Perhaps they thought that they could actually rally together as one, live as they chose, and keep God from judging the earth again -- even though God had promised that He would never judge the earth with *water* again. After the flood waters dried up, God put a rainbow into the sky as a token of this promise, and rainbows have been appearing in the sky all over the world ever since. Apparently though, the descendants of Noah did not trust this promise. Under the leadership of a man named Nimrod, the people began to build a big tower that would reach into heaven, perhaps to the very throne of God. If God should send another flood, they could escape by climbing up into the tower. This tower would be located in their capital city, which was later known as Babylon. (Remember that name.) The narrative of what happened is given in Genesis 11:1-9: "Now the whole earth used the same language and the same words. It came about as they journeyed east, that they found a plain in the land of Shinar and settled there. They said to one another, 'Come, let us make bricks and burn *them* thoroughly.' And they used brick for stone, and they used tar for mortar. They said, 'Come, let us build for ourselves a city, and a tower whose top *will reach* into heaven, and let us make for ourselves a name, otherwise we will be scattered abroad over the face of the whole earth.' The Lord came down to see the city and the tower which the sons of men had built. The Lord said, 'Behold, they are one people, and they all have the same language. And this is what they began to do, and now nothing which they purpose to do will be impossible for them. Come, let Us go down and there confuse their language, so that they will not understand one another's speech.' So the Lord scattered them abroad from there over the face of the whole earth; and they stopped building the city. Therefore its name was called Babel, because there the Lord confused the language of the whole earth; and from there the Lord scattered them abroad over the face of the whole earth."

Today we live in a world of worker's unions. The United Mine Workers have unionized against the mine owners to get more pay and benefits and better working conditions. The United Steelworkers have united against the owners of the steel companies for the same reasons. (This is by no means a statement against organized labor- just a comparison.) The thing that is so preposterous is when people try to organize against *God*. Did Nimrod and his followers really believe they could build a tower that would reach into heaven?

Apparently so. This belief has been christened "the spirit of Babylon." This spirit is an attempt, which began in Nimrod's day but continues today, to establish a one-world religion and government. It wants man, not God, as the head. Man can reach heaven all by his lonesome. "The spirit of Babylon" has caused man to doubt God's promises and attempt to change His laws and statues. This is described in Psalms chapter 2:

"Why are the nations in an uproar
And the peoples devising a vain thing?
The kings of the earth take their stand
And the rulers take counsel together
Against the Lord and against His Anointed, saying,
'Let us tear their fetters apart
And cast away their cords from us!'
He who sits in the heavens laughs,
The Lord scoffs at them.
Then He will speak to them in His anger
And terrify them in His fury, saying,
'But as for Me, I have installed My King
Upon Zion, My holy mountain.'
'I will surely tell of the decree of the Lord:
He said to Me, "You are My Son,
Today I have begotten You.
"Ask of Me, and I will surely give the nations as Your inheritance,
And the *very* ends of the earth as Your possession.
"You shall break them with a rod of iron,
You shall shatter them like earthenware."'
Now therefore, O kings, show discernment;

Take warning, O judges of the earth.
Worship the Lord with reverence
And rejoice with trembling.
Do homage to the Son, that He not become angry, and you
perish *in* the way,
For His wrath may soon be kindled.
How blessed are all who take refuge in Him!"

So it seems like Nimrod and his people were not taking refuge in God, but in their own abilities. God said, "Come, let Us (notice "Us" is plural and not singular -- the Godhead Three in One is involved.) go down and there confuse their language." (11:7) The confusing of languages forced the people to move out across the earth – to finally do what God had told them to do in the first place. Genesis 10 gives a genealogy overview of what would happen in Chapter 11: "From these the coastlands of the nations were separated into their lands, every one according to his language, according to their families, into their nations. The descendants of Shem, Ham, and Japheth moved out in different directions. Obviously every person that has been born on the earth has descended from one of these three boys.

Our Messiah would descend from Shem.

Chapter 18

The Remarkable Story of Abraham

The first 11 chapters of Genesis cover about 2,000 years. It seems as though God is in a hurry to get to a most important chapter and a most important story, the story of Abraham. Short and sweet -- after Noah and his family got off the ark, Shem had a son, Arpachshad, then he had a son and he had a son and on and on, all the way through the generations until we come to Abraham, or "Abram" as he was known at first. (God then slows down and has the rest of the Old Testament covering a period of 2,000 more years.)

Abram's name means "exalted father," but in the beginning, he was not a father at all. His wife's name was Sarai and she was barren. God had promised Abram that if he would leave his home country and travel to a land that he had never seen before, He would use Abram's own son to follow his father in the line to the Messiah.

In Chapter 12 it states,
"Now the Lord said to Abram,
'Go forth from your country,
And from your relatives
And from your father's house,
To the land which I will show you;
And I will make you a great nation,
And I will bless you,
And make your name great;
And so you shall be a blessing;
And I will bless those who bless you,
And the one who curses you I will curse.
And in you all the families of the earth will be blessed ... To your descendants I will give this land."
Abram naturally wondered how this could be, but God made a promise to Abram, "One who will come forth from your own body, he shall be your heir." (Genesis 15:4)

To make this promise "official," God made a covenant with Abram in Genesis 15:5-18: "And He took him outside and said, 'Now look toward the heavens, and count the stars, if you are able to count them.' And He said to him, 'So shall your descendants be.' Then he believed in the Lord; and He reckoned it to him as righteousness. And He said to him, 'I am the Lord who brought you out of Ur of the Chaldeans, to give you this land to possess it.' He said, 'O Lord God, how may I know that I will possess it?' So He said to him, 'Bring Me a three year old heifer, and a three year old female goat, and a three year old ram, and a turtledove, and a young pigeon.'

Then he brought all these to Him and cut them in two, and laid each half opposite the other; but he did not cut the birds. The birds of prey came down upon the carcasses, and Abram drove them away. Now when the sun was going down, a deep sleep fell upon Abram; and behold, terror *and* great darkness fell upon him. *God* said to Abram, 'Know for certain that your descendants will be strangers in a land that is not theirs, where they will be enslaved and oppressed four hundred years. But I will also judge the nation whom they will serve, and afterward they will come out with many possessions. As for you, you shall go to your fathers in peace; you will be buried at a good old age. Then in the fourth generation they will return here, for the iniquity of the Amorite is not yet complete.' It came about when the sun had set, that it was very dark, and behold, *there appeared* a smoking oven and a flaming torch which passed between these pieces. On that day the Lord made a covenant with Abram, saying, 'To your descendants I have given this land, From the river of Egypt as far as the great river, the river Euphrates'."

The *way* God made His covenant with Abram is the most important thing that God did to insure his covenant would be fulfilled. In Abram's day, the way two people agreed upon a covenant was to cut an animal in half, hold hands and walk between the pieces. When they did that together, it meant that each one promised he would keep his part of what had been agreed upon. In this covenant God made with Abram, God walked through *all by Himself*. Abram was asleep when God went through. This meant that God alone would be responsible for keeping his covenant.

It did not depend upon the conduct or faithfulness of Abram, which is a good thing.

In the New Testament, Abraham is known as the "father of the faithful", but he was not very faithful at first. Before the covenant, Abraham had failed God when he left his home that God had placed him in because a famine had occurred. Instead of trusting God to take care of him, he moved down into Egypt. While there, he lied to Pharaoh about Sarai being his wife, and told Pharaoh that she was his sister, fearing for his life. Sometime later, he left Egypt. Years after that, God made the covenant with him. Abram proved unfaithful again when he stayed a while in Gerar. (Genesis 20) Here again, he lied about Sarai being his wife, claiming she was his sister, again fearing for his life. He had not yet learned to trust God to take care of him. In both cases God personally intervened to keep a very tragic thing from happening. If Abram's conduct had been part of the covenant, then he would certainly not have kept up his end of the bargain.

The Messiah will next come through Abraham.

Chapter 19

God Reconfirms His Covenant with Abraham

In Genesis 17:3-4, God appeared to Abram to reconfirm the covenant He had made back in Chapter 12 and 15. Abram fell on his face before God and listened to God speak. God said (and I am paraphrasing here), "My covenant is with you. You will be the father of a multitude of nations. You and Sarai will have a son in your old age. Through the one born, I will make you a father of a multitude. From now on your name will be Abraham which means a father of a multitude." God also went on to change Abraham's wife's name from Sarai to Sarah. God said that she would be the mother of kings and mighty nations.

When Abram was 99 years old, God finally changed his name to Abraham. About a year later, in Genesis 17:17-22, "Abraham fell on his face and laughed, and said in his heart, 'Will a child be born to a man one hundred years old? And will Sarah, who is ninety years old, bear *a child*?' And Abraham said to God, 'Oh that Ishmael (Hold on, we're coming to him) might live before You!' But God said, 'No, but Sarah your wife will bear you a son, and you shall call his name Isaac; and I will establish My covenant with him for an everlasting covenant for his descendants after him. As for Ishmael, I have heard you; behold, I will bless him, and will make him fruitful and will multiply him exceedingly. He shall become the father of twelve princes, and I will make him a great nation. But My covenant I will establish with Isaac, whom Sarah will bear to you at this season next year.' When He finished talking with him, God went up from Abraham."

Ishmael was the product of a pagan custom of that day. According to the Code of Hammurabi, a well-preserved Babylonian law code of ancient Mesopotamia dating back to about 1754 BC, if a wife was barren, her husband could take his wife's handmaid and bear a child through her. So, at Sarah's suggestion, Abraham took Hagar, Sarah's maid, and they had a son through her and named him Ishmael. Later on, Abraham asked that Ishmael would be his heir, but God said, "No"; one born from Sarah in her old age would be the one to fulfill the covenant God made with Abraham. Sometime later, Sarah bore a son as God promised. They named him Isaac as God had told them to. The name Isaac means "laughter." Both Abraham and Sarah laughed when God told them they would have a son when she was old. "Sarah said, 'God has made laughter for me; everyone who hears will laugh with me.' And she said, 'Who would have said to Abraham that Sarah would nurse children? Yet I have borne him a son in his old age.' The child grew and was weaned, and Abraham made a great feast on the day that Isaac was weaned." (21:6-8)

The birth of Ishmael would cause problems in Abraham's family in that he would be a legal heir along with Isaac. On that feast of weaning day, Ishmael was seen mocking Isaac. Sarah really took drastic measures by ordering Hagar and Ishmael out of the house. (This retaliation, too, was permitted in the Code of Hammurabi.) Sarah intended to make sure that the son of her handmaid would not inherit Abraham's property. Sarah is not one of the nicer persons in the Bible. On two occasions she cooperated with Abraham by pretending to be his sister, she laughed at God when God said she would bear a son in her old age, and it was *her* big idea to give Hagar to Abraham to start with. Now, she ordered Abraham to send Ishmael and his mom out into the desert where there was no chance for them to survive —which is probably what she intended.

So, Abraham complied with Sarah's wishes and sent Hagar and Ishmael away with just a skin of water and a loaf of bread. Abraham was very distressed to do this because he loved Ishmael, but God assured Abraham that He would take care of the boy and he would make a mighty nation of him.

Hagar and Ishmael went out across the desert toward Egypt. When they had used the last of their water, Hagar placed Ishmael under a bush and sat down a distance from him because she could not bear to see him die. God heard Ishmael's crying and provided comfort by letting them see a well of water. With renewed strength and the Lord's provisions, they made it down into Egypt.

Hagar found Ishmael an Egyptian wife and he became the father of twelve princes.

The promised heir, Isaac, would be the next specific person in the line to the Messiah.

Chapter 20

The Destruction of Sodom and Gomorrah

Abraham had a nephew named Lot. At one point, these men had so many possessions, like flocks and herds of animals along with tents, that their herdsmen started arguing. Abraham did not want to have a family squabble, so he told Nephew Lot that he could have the pick of the pastures. Lot chose the valley land around Sodom and moved into its cities. (Wrong choice!)

One day 3 men came to visit Abraham and Sarah. They once again promised a flesh and blood son to the couple. Who were these 3 men, you may ask? Well, two were angels and one was the Lord Himself. Abraham fed them and then this happened: "The men rose up from there, and looked down toward Sodom; and Abraham was walking with them to send them off. The Lord said, 'Shall I hide from Abraham what I am about to do, since Abraham will surely become a great and mighty nation, and in him all the nations of the earth will be blessed? For I have chosen him, so that he may command his children and his household after him to keep the way of the Lord by doing righteousness and justice, so that the Lord may bring upon Abraham what He has spoken about him.'

And the Lord said, 'The outcry of Sodom and Gomorrah is indeed great, and their sin is exceedingly grave. I will go down now, and see if they have done entirely according to its outcry, which has come to Me; and if not, I will know'." (Genesis 18:16-21)

Abraham tried to intercede for the people of Sodom, after all, his nephew Lot and his family lived there. Abraham asked God if He would spare the city if He found 50 righteous people in it. God said that He would spare the city for the sake of 50. Abraham carefully and maybe a little fearfully kept on. Would God save the city for 45 righteous people? God said that He would. Abraham kept on speaking very carefully and respectfully, coming down with the numbers – 40 then 30 then 20 and stopping at 10. God said He would spare the city for as few as 10 people. Why did Abraham stop at 10? Lot had a wife, two daughters, sons, and future sons-in-law there (19:12-14), plus, surely Lot would have won over other people.

Chapter 19:1 says: "Now the two angels came to Sodom in the evening as Lot was sitting in the gate of Sodom." Sometimes angels take on the appearance of men when they come to earth to do a service for God. The angels' intention was to spend the night in the city square, but Lot was insistent that they spend the night inside his house. He prepared a feast for them, and baked unleavened bread, and they ate. If lot had hoped the people in the city would not find out about these men, he was sorely disappointed. Chapter 19:4-11 shows how perverted and wicked the people of Sodom and Gomorrah were: "Before they lay down, the men of the city, the men of Sodom, surrounded the house, both young and old, all the people from every quarter; and they called to Lot and said to him, 'Where are the men who came to you tonight? Bring them out to us that we may have relations with them.' But Lot went out to them at the doorway, and shut the door behind him, and said, 'Please, my brothers, do not act wickedly. Now behold, I have two daughters who have not had relations with man; please let me bring them out to you, and do to them whatever you like; only do nothing to these men, inasmuch as they have come under the shelter of my roof.' But they said, 'Stand aside.' Furthermore, they said, 'This one came in as an alien, and already he is acting like a judge; now we will treat you worse than them.' So they pressed hard against Lot and came near to break the door. But the men reached out their hands and brought Lot into the house with them, and shut the door. They struck the men who were at the doorway of the house with blindness, both small and great, so that they wearied *themselves trying* to find the doorway."

What in the world was Lot thinking when he offered his daughters to these perverted men? Those girls would have been horribly raped and probably used as a ransom to force the angels to come out. We know the two angels were more than a match for all the people in the city; they finally stepped in and took charge by smiting the sodomites with blindness.

The next morning the angels told Lot to get his family out of the city and into the mountains as they could not destroy the city until his family had left (So much for 10 righteous people). Lot's two sons-in-law just scoffed at him and refused to get out. Lot, himself, was reluctant to leave so the two angels had to take him and his wife and two daughters by the hands and lead them out. They told Lot and his family to flee to the mountains and not look back. Lot's wife did look back and turned into a pillar of salt. Lot and his daughters first went to a small city called Zoar, then left there and went into the mountains to a cave.

What happened later in the cave would cause me to wonder if Lot was at all righteous if not for what Peter said in 2 Peter 2:2-10: "And *if* He rescued righteous Lot, oppressed by the sensual conduct of unprincipled men (for by what he saw and heard *that* righteous man, while living among them, felt *his* righteous soul tormented day after day by *their* lawless deeds), *then* the Lord knows how to rescue the godly from temptation, and to keep the unrighteous under punishment for the day of judgment, and especially those who indulge the flesh in *its* corrupt desires and despise authority." What happened in the cave (I say again!) is really unbelievable. Lot's daughters committed incest with their own father, thinking to preserve their family line. The immorality they saw and lived with from day to day must have really corrupted their minds. This is another example of the corrupt moral codes of this time in history, but even the Code of Hammurabi punished incest with death. The Bible tells what happened: The older daughter got him drunk and laid with him that night. The next night the younger did the same thing to their father. He was so drunk that he never knew what happened. Nine months later, the firstborn had a son and named him Moab and he became the father of the Moabites. The younger daughter also had a son and he became the father of the sons of Ammon.

A Moabite girl named Ruth would one day play a very significant role in keeping the line to the Messiah alive. Her story is told in the book of Ruth. By God's providence, she became the great grandmother of King David.

Chapter 21

Abraham Tested

One of the great chapters in the Bible is Genesis 22. In it we see a picture of what would one day happen to Christ, our Messiah. Verses 1 and 2 say, "Now it came about after these things, that God tested Abraham, and said to him, 'Abraham!' And he said, 'Here I am.' He said, 'Take now your son, your only son, whom you love, Isaac, and go to the land of Moriah, and offer him there as a burnt offering on one of the mountains of which I will tell you'." (WHAT?) Abraham obediently took Isaac and two of his young servants and prepared for the three day trip to the exact spot that God had told him. He split wood for the burnt offering before he left and carried it with him rather than waiting to cut it when he got there.

When he got near the place of which God had spoken, he took Isaac and the split wood for the offering and told the young men to wait with the donkey while Isaac and he went to worship God. He told the young men that he and Isaac would be back. (How could both of them return if he followed through and offered Isaac as a burnt sacrifice?)

Abraham had every intention of doing what God told him to do. Isaac, obviously not knowing what was about to happen, said, "'My father!' And he (Abraham) said, 'Here I am, my son.' And he said, 'Behold, the fire and the wood, but where is the lamb for the burnt offering?' Abraham said, 'God will provide for Himself the lamb for the burnt offering, my son.' So the two of them walked on together. Then they came to the place of which God had told him; and Abraham built the altar there and arranged the wood, and bound his son Isaac and laid him on the altar, on top of the wood. Abraham stretched out his hand and took the knife to slay his son. But the angel of the Lord called to him from heaven and said, 'Abraham, Abraham!' And he said, 'Here I am.' He said, 'Do not stretch out your hand against the lad, and do nothing to him; for now I know that you fear God, since you have not withheld your son, your only son, from Me'."

What if Abraham had followed through and killed his son? And how did he know that he and Isaac would return to the young men who were waiting with the donkeys? Remember that Isaac was the next in line on the road leading to the promised Messiah. All the promises that God had made to Abraham about being the father of a mighty nation were to be fulfilled through Isaac. But if Isaac was dead, how could God's promises be fulfilled? What exactly was going on in Abraham's mind as he prepared to kill Isaac? Hebrews 11:17-19 gives us the answer: "By faith Abraham, when he was tested, offered up Isaac, and he who had received the promises was offering up his only begotten *son*; *it was he* to whom it was said, 'In Isaac your descendants shall be called.' *He considered that God is able to raise people even from the dead, from which he also received him back as a type."*

So, Abraham told Isaac that God Himself would provide a lamb for the burnt offering. But, God did not provide a lamb on that day. Instead, God provided a ram for the burnt offering. About two thousand years later, God did provide a lamb, Who would die for the sins of the world. This lamb was God's only Son, Jesus, who left His glorious place in heaven to give His life for us so we would not have to spend eternity separated from God, paying for our sins. God spared Abraham from sacrificing his only son, Isaac. God did not spare his only begotten Son and allowed him to be crucified on a cross and to give up his life for sinful humanity.

Chapter 23 records the death of Sarah. She died in Hebron in the land that God promised to Abraham and his descendants. After a few days spent mourning and weeping for her, Abraham got up to make arrangements for her burial. Abraham did not own any land of his own, so he bought a piece of land complete with a cave in which he buried his wife. She had been a strong woman for Abraham, though both of them had committed mistakes and acts of unbelief. We all are guilty of these things, but if we belong to God, we will learn lessons that will strengthen our faith. Notice that Genesis records no objections from Sarah when Abraham took Isaac to sacrifice him. It is not how you start out in life but how you finish which is most important. Sarah is described in Hebrews 11:11 as a woman of faith.

The verse says, "By faith even Sarah herself received ability to conceive, even beyond the proper time of life, since she considered Him faithful who had promised." The birth of Isaac was a miracle as Sarah was far too old to have a baby. About 2000 years later, there was another birth. The mother was a young virgin girl named Mary. The Holy Spirit came upon her and caused her to conceive and a child was born. Remember back in Genesis 3:15? This verse stated that the seed of a woman would be born. No man was in involved in her pregnancy. Miraculously, she gave birth to the One who was promised by God Himself. This Son would crush the head of the serpent and live a perfect life so that he would be able to die for the sin of the world. This man, who was born in Bethlehem, was the only begotten son of God, as Isaac was the only promised son of Abraham.

Chapter 22

A Bride For Isaac

With Sarah gone, Abraham knew that Isaac needed a wife. Isaac's offspring would carry on his lineage – the lineage to the Messiah. Genesis 24:1-9 records Abraham's instructions on how to accomplish this:

"Now Abraham was old, advanced in age; and the LORD had blessed Abraham in every way. Abraham said to his servant, the oldest of his household, who had charge of all that he owned, 'Please place your hand under my thigh, and I will make you swear by the LORD, the God of heaven and the God of earth, that you shall not take a wife for my son from the daughters of the Canaanites, among whom I live, but you will go to my country and to my relatives, and take a wife for my son Isaac.' The servant said to him, 'Suppose the woman is not willing to follow me to this land; should I take your son back to the land from where you came?' Then Abraham said to him, 'Beware that you do not take my son back there! The LORD, the God of heaven, who took me from my father's house and from the land of my birth, and who spoke to me and who swore to me, saying, "To your descendants I will give this land," He will send His angel before you, and you will take a wife for my son from there. But if the woman is not willing to follow you, then you will be free from this my oath; only do not take my son back there. So the servant placed his hand under the thigh of Abraham his master, and swore to him concerning this matter."

Abraham's servant prepared for a long trip to Mesopotamia, some 450 miles away. Mesopotamia was the land in which Abraham had grown up and a lot of his relatives still lived there. Abraham did not want Isaac marrying a girl from the pagans who lived around him in his present home.

Abraham deeded this tremendous undertaking to his top servant, the one he trusted the most. The servant, whose name we are not given, loaded 10 camels with a variety of gifts of gold and all kinds of jewelry. He no idea about the people he would encounter, if they would accept him and if there would even be a girl there fit to be Isaac's wife. This was an important mission.

God was the One who instituted marriage way back in the Garden when God prepared a wife for Adam and preformed their marriage Himself. If people would wait upon God, He has a mate for every man and woman that He gifts to be married. The servant did not know it, but there *was* a girl that God had chosen for Isaac. She is mentioned in 24:15. Her name was Rebecca, the daughter of Bethuel, Abraham's cousin. In those days, it was customary for someone to marry their cousin.

How does a person know the one God has chosen for them? Abraham's servant prayed that God would make this known to him. So, follow the servant's example and pray and wait on God. Also, the servant depended on divine providence. Webster's dictionary defines "providence" as an event that or act that is attributed to God. God was to control the events that would lead the servant to the girl God had already chosen. The servant went to a well where he knew young girls would come to draw water. He hoped that one of these girls would be the right one. The servant prayed that God would let him know by asking for a sign. What happened is given in chapter 24:12–14:

"He said, 'O LORD, the God of my master Abraham, please grant me success today, and show lovingkindness to my master Abraham. Behold, I am standing by the spring, and the daughters of the men of the city are coming out to draw water; now may it be that the girl to whom I say, "Please let down your jar so that I may drink," and who answers, "Drink, and I will water your camels also", may she be the one whom You have appointed for Your servant Isaac; and by this I will know that You have shown lovingkindness to my master'."

Before he had finished his prayer, Rebecca came out to the well, carrying her pitcher on her shoulder. The Bible says that she was a beautiful girl and still a virgin. The servant went up to her and asked if could have a drink. She lowered the pitcher to the man and he drank. She also watered all of his camels. After she finished, he rewarded her with some expensive gifts and asked whose daughter she was and if they had room for him and the camels to spend the night. She replied that she was the daughter of Bethuel the son of Milcah, the son of Nahor. Nahor was Abraham's brother. She said there was plenty of room, and ran off, leaving him standing there.

The servant took this time to bow his head and thank God for His kindness in leading him to the household of Abraham's brother --- divine providence! He blessed the God of Abraham for his lovingkindness and truth to Abraham. When the girl got home, she spoke to her relatives about the man and showed the gifts the he had given her. Now Rebecca had a brother named Laban, and when he saw the gifts and heard about the man, he ran out to meet him. Laban offered the man a place for his camels and also a room and food for Abraham's servant.

Before the servant would even touch his food, he said he needed to tell them of his mission. Briefly, he told them that he was from the house of Abraham, seeking a bride for Isaac. The servant told them about his covenant with Abraham and of his mission to find a bride in the land where his relatives dwelt. Then he told how Rebecca had given him water and watered his camels also. He said God had answered his prayer, and Rebecca was the one God had chosen.

Her family agreed that this was of God and they would not stand in her way if she agreed to go with the man. So, they asked Rebecca if she was willing to return with this man and she replied, "Yes." Her family wanted them to delay their leaving for a couple of weeks, but the servant said it was urgent that they start back immediately. The next day, she and Abraham's servant left with her family's blessing. Imagine what the trip back would be like as Rebecca knew nothing about Isaac or the country to which she was going. Imagine, as they sat around the camp fire at night, the servant telling her about Abraham and about the covenant that God had made with him. He would have told her about the miraculous birth of Isaac as Sarah, who had been barren all her life, had given birth to him in her old age. He would relay the story of how Abraham was willing to sacrifice Isaac as a burnt offering just because God had told him to. He might dramatically recount the moment that Abraham lifted up his knife to plunge it into the heart of Isaac (and she would have screamed at this point), and how God had called his name telling him not to do it. Rebecca would learn that God had been testing Abraham, and at that exact moment knew that Abraham feared Him.

When Jesus ascended from this world to Heaven about 2,000 years ago, He promised to send the Holy Spirit or Comforter back. In Acts 2, the Holy Spirit came. Since that day, the Spirit has been seeking a bride for the Lord Jesus Christ. She is sometimes called "the church" or "the body of Christ." The Bride of Christ is made up of all nations and races of people. An individual becomes part of the Bride of Christ when he or she believes in the name of Jesus Christ. One day Jesus will return in the air to take His bride, made up of both living and dead believers, into Heaven. My mother died the day before Mother's Day in 2014. It was a very sad time and she is missed by the family she left behind. We were planning a family reunion for her but God took her to Heaven to spend Mother's Day with her mother. I do know that one day we will be together again in a place where there will be no more suffering and death. The Apostle Paul encourages us in 1 Thessalonians 4:13-18: "But we do not want you to be uninformed, brethren, about those who are asleep, so that you will not grieve as do the rest who have no hope. For if we believe that Jesus died and rose again, even so God will bring with Him those who have fallen asleep in Jesus. For this we say to you by the word of the Lord, that we who are alive and remain until the coming of the Lord, will not precede those who have fallen asleep. For the Lord Himself will descend from heaven with a shout, with the voice of *the* archangel and with the trumpet of God, and the dead in Christ will rise first. Then we who are alive and remain will be caught up together with them in the clouds to meet the Lord in the air, and so we shall always be with the Lord. Therefore comfort one another with these words."

One day Isaac was standing by a well late in the evening. He was lonesome and hurting as they had recently buried his mother. He looked up and saw the camels coming. Rebecca saw him and jumped down off her mount in great excitement. She asked Abraham's servant, "Who is that man coming to meet us." The servant replied, "He is my master." Rebecca took off her veil and covered herself. She finally met her husband-to-be. Genesis says that Isaac took her into his mother's tent and he loved her, and they were married. Isaac was comforted over the death of his mother.

Chapter 25 records the death of Abraham; he had lived 175 years. Both Isaac and Ishmael were there to bury him in the same cave in which Abraham had buried Sarah, the only land that Abraham owned. Even though he was a nomad, wandering from place to place, he lived and died as a very rich man in his day. He could have bought a whole lot of land if he had chosen to. Why did he not do that? Hebrews 11:9,10 says this: "By faith he lived as an alien in the land of promise, as in a foreign land dwelling in tents with Isaac and Jacob, fellow heirs of the same promise; for he was looking for the city which has foundations whose builder and maker was God."

The road to the Messiah will be continued through the promised son, Isaac, his wife, Rebecca, and one born to them that God Himself will choose.

Chapter 23

A Biblical Response

So, how should you respond to all the information we have discussed in this book? Perhaps you attend a public school, community college, or university and you are not being taught the things of God. Many of your teachers or professors will present the evolution theory and many other theories and philosophies that you know are not true. In order to pass some of your courses, you will have to write papers and take exams in which you will be required respond to or regurgitate information. You may ask yourself, am I disobeying God in this? I don't think so. The things I learned in high school biology have only made me more aware of the truth and reality of creation. The time I spent in college studying the laws of electricity and refrigeration made me see that there is order in God's universe. You may have to give the answers that teachers and professors expect, but in both public and private conversations, let your beliefs be known in a humble, understanding way. Make sure you stay in frequent contact with believing parents and have a supportive church family. Make sure you read and study the Bible as often as you can, preferably on a daily basis. Pray daily for your instructors, the evolution scientists, and other young people who are having to make the same choices as you.

You may be a teacher of elementary, junior high, or high school students. You may be a college or university professor. How do you respond? You have such a great responsibility. You not only influence the young people you teach, but it trickles down to their children and their children. Be as "wise as serpents and harmless as doves." (Matthew 10:16)

Last, but certainly not least, you may be the parent of a young person that you teach yourself or send off to school each day or you have dropped off at a university. If you homeschool, you can control what your children are taught. If you take them or send them, you are entrusting your treasure to instructors you may not know. You may not know their background or beliefs. What do you do? Place yourself and/or your children in the hands of a mighty God. "Now to Him who is able to keep you from stumbling, and to make you stand in the presence of His glory blameless with great joy, to the only God our Savior, through Jesus Christ our Lord, *be* glory, majesty, dominion and authority, before all time and now and forever. Amen. (Jude 24)

Do you remember the chronicle of Daniel and his three Hebrew friends: Hananiah, Mishael and Azariah? They were young men back in 605 B.C., probably teenagers, who, along with many other young people (and older folks), were captured by the invading Babylonian army. The first chapter of Daniel says all the young people were "youths in whom was no defect, who were good-looking, showing intelligence in every *branch of* wisdom, endowed with understanding and discerning knowledge, and who had ability for serving in the king's court; and *he* (Nebuchadnezzar, king of Babylon) ordered him (Ashpenaz, the chief of the officials) to teach them the literature and language of the Chaldeans." They were taken from their royal and prominent families, from their homeland of Judah, and into a strange and faraway country.   King Nebuchadnezzar "appointed for them a daily ration from the king's choice food and from the wine which he drank, and *appointed* that they should be educated three years, at the end of which they were to enter the king's personal service." Ashpenaz even changed their names to some of Babylon's pagan gods in order to further separate them from their home, their customs, and their God. But......."for these four youths, God gave them knowledge and intelligence in every *branch of* literature and wisdom; Daniel even understood all *kinds of* visions and dreams." At the end of their educational training, King Nebuchadnezzar "talked with them, and out of them all not one was found like Daniel, Hananiah, Mishael and Azariah; so they entered the king's personal service.   As for every matter of wisdom and understanding about which the king consulted them, he found them ten times better than all the magicians *and* conjurers who *were* in all his realm."

Because they had been taught about and believed in God, these young people were able to stand in and withstand an ungodly and idolatrous nation. Most likely they were terribly homesick so they formed a bond among themselves that would help keep them rooted and righteous. Instead of Daniel and his friends being brainwashed, they brought the one true God to Babylon, they influenced a king and culture that ruled the world. The pagan teachings they were forced to learn did not keep them from being loyal to their God; it actually caused their theology to be stronger. A day came when King Nebuchadnezzar was dedicating the huge, golden statue he had made. The Babylonian people were being forced to bow down and worship this idol. (Chapter 3) The penalty for refusing to do this was to be thrown into a fiery furnace. (Gulp!) But Hananiah, Mishael, and Azariah refused to bow, and as a result they were tied up tightly and thrown, not into the fiery furnace, but into the (1)fiery, (2)blazing, (3)scorching, (4)burning, (5)blistering, (6)sweltering, (7)flaming furnace --- heated seven times hotter than normal ! (Double gulp!) They fell down in the flames and what? Screamed for help? Burned up? Nope. Nebuchadnezzar looked into the furnace and was amazed to see four men walking around unharmed. God was there with His faithful servants! God honored his servants by going in *with* them. "Come out ... and Come here!" the king commanded. He looked at them and their clothes were not burnt even a little. He smelled of them and they did not stink like smoke. He thought, "Hair singes easily; let's look at that." Nope. Nope. Nope. Their clothes were not burnt; they did not smell; their hair was not singed. By their courage, they had won over the heart of a pagan king who proclaimed "How great are His (the good Lord's) signs and how mighty are his wonders! His kingdom is an everlasting kingdom and His dominion is from generation to generation."

That's what happened to Daniel's 3 faithful friends -- Daniel must have been out of town on a kingly errand that day. But, it soon came his turn. Would he stand up for His beliefs? In Chapter 6, Daniel was cast into a den of lions for praying to God when he was supposed to only pray to the king. The king was devastated when he knew he had been tricked into making this law and that his faithful employee was doomed – it seemed. But, God kept him safe – no bite marks and no broken bones from having been dropped into the den. Now, this was a different king – not Nebuchadnezzar. Nebuchadnezzar had been changed by these 4 boys who had been violently jerked from their comfortable home and way of life. They had endured the test of homesickness and a completely different culture with strange foods, a plethora of idols to worship, and a bunch of so-called friends that were only out to make them fail.

I read about a high school kid who outwardly had everything going for him. He had rich parents who gave him everything he wanted. He drove an expensive car and wore the most expensive clothes money could buy. He was very popular in school because he threw lavish parties. He really knew how to live it up. But (and again, there is always a but) deep inside he was miserable and empty. The things of this world could not bring him peace or happiness. He was at the point of committing suicide, but there was a girl in school who was different. She wore no fancy clothes, had no car, nor did she have a lot of the things this world had to offer. But (and there is always a good but) she had a peace about her that surpassed all understanding. Before the young went through with his plan to commit suicide, he decided to talk to her and ask why she was so different. She explained that she had a personal relationship with Jesus, the Messiah. To this he replied, "I have tried religion and it never worked for me." She explained that she was not religious but she had accepted Jesus into her life and He filled all her inner needs. She explained the gospel to him and he became a believer in Jesus. People are watching Christians if what they profess is real.

First Peter 3:15 says, "Sanctify Christ as Lord in your hearts, always ready to make a defense to everyone who asks you to give an account for the hope that is in you, yet with gentleness and reverence.

Bibliography

Bergman, J. (1997). Unraveling DNA's Design. Retrieved from http://www.khouse.org/articles/1997/143/

Courtesy of University of Liverpool Faculty of Health & Life Sciences. Walking skeleton from Andrew Bell, Anatomia Britannica (1770s-1780s). (2013, November 12). Retrieved from https://www.flickr.com/photos/liverpoolhls/10818431486?text=skeleton. License at https://creativecommons.org/licenses/by-sa/2.0/legalcode. No changes made. Accessed September 30, 2015.

God of Creation [Motion picture on VHS]. (1998). United States: Moody Video.

Johnson, Phillip. "The Fact of Evolution." *Darwin on Trial*. 2nd ed. Downers Grove: InterVarsity, 1993. 70. Print.

Looking for Life: Carl Sagan with Ted Koppel. (1996). ABC's Nightline.

MacArthur, J. (1999). *Battle for the Beginning*. Nashville, Tennessee: Thomas Nelson.

McGraw, K. (Photographer). (2011, January 14). Peacock on Table [digital image]. Retrieved from https://www.flickr.com/photos/4blogs/5371485515. License at https://creativecommons.org/licenses/by-sa/2.0/legalcode. No changes made. Accessed September 30, 2015.

Miller, J. (2011). The Five Manifestations of Natural

Phenomena: Apologetics Press.

Norkum, M. (Photographer). (2015, June 30). Northern Flicker feeding babies [digital image]. Retrieved from https://www.flickr.com/photos/mikenorkum/19308380691. License at https://creativecommons.org/licenses/by-nd/2.0/legalcode. No changes made. Accessed September 30, 2015.

Romans 1:21-32 | Thru the Bible with Dr. J. Vernon McGee. (n.d.). Retrieved 2015.

Salvagnin, U. (Photographer). (2010, May 14). Honey bee swarm [digital image]. Retrieved from https://www.flickr.com/photos/kaibara/4632384645/in/photolist. License at https://creativecommons.org/licenses/by-sa/2.0/legalcode. No changes made. Accessed September 30, 2015.

Shaffern, R. (2009). *Antiquity to Enlightenment* (p. 3). Lanham, Maryland: Rowman and Littlefield.

Signposts Aloft [Motion picture on VHS]. (1998). United States: Moody.Today's Creation Moment transcripts. www.creationmoments.com. Used by permission.

The Virtual Nature Trail at Penn State New Kensington. (2014). Retrieved from http://www.psu.edu/dept/nkbiology/naturetrail/speciespages/whitetaileddeer

Why Animal Rights? (2015). Retrieved from http://www.peta.org/about-peta/why-peta/why-animal-rights/